Credit Where Credit is Due

The Evolution of Business

Banking in Ireland

An Insight
by
Frank Casey

Institute of Public Administration
Dublin

First published 2000
by the Institute of Public Administration
57 - 61 Lansdowne Road
Dublin 4
Ireland
for
ICC Bank plc

British Library Cataloguing in Publication Data

ISBN 1 902448 41 3

Cover design by Butler Claffey Design

Index by Brigid Pike

Typeset by Artwerk

Printed by Criterion Press

CREDIT WHERE CREDIT IS DUE

This book is due for return on or before the last date shown below.

*To my wife Alison whose help, advice and
encouragement made the writing of this
book such a pleasurable task.*

Contents

Foreword

ICC Bank has played a pivotal role in the evolution of Irish business since 1933. Since then many entrepreneurs and business ideas have successfully passed through the Bank's hands. Some of these have succeeded internationally on a scale unimaginable to their founding fathers; many are operating successfully on a more modest scale while others have given rise to exciting new business offshoots.

ICC Bank has always looked favourably on a sound proposal backed by a dedicated and competent promoter. We acknowledge and admire the hard work and dedication of these entrepreneurs and their part in building the skills base that has made Ireland one of the most rapidly growing economies in the industrialised world.

Having spent over forty years of his working life in ICC Bank, including twenty-two years as chief executive, Frank Casey is in a unique position to reflect on the evolution of Irish industrial and commercial development over the decades. In this book he reminisces on the part played by ICC Bank and the business community in this transformation.

It is interesting to note that, almost seventy years after its founding, ICC Bank's original capital markets operations have once again found a prominent role in the funding of business in modern Ireland through the Bank's much expanded venture capital activities.

The achievements of the Irish economy and ICC Bank are closely associated. We, in ICC Bank, look forward to continuing this successful partnership with Irish business into the new millennium.

Michael Quinn
Managing Director
ICC Bank

Acknowledgements

This book does not purport to be an economic or historical treatise. There are many professional economists and historians who have dealt more than adequately with Ireland's economic history. Nor is the book a formal history of ICC Bank. Much of it is personal reminiscence, although I had the benefit of archival material, including minutes of ICC board meetings and annual general meetings, for the early years. I am also indebted to members of the present ICC staff for information about the years since I retired in 1991.

In writing this book I have been helped by so many people that there is a danger I will omit some who should have been mentioned. If that has happened, I offer my apologies to those concerned.

In ICC I received great help and encouragement from the managing director Michael Quinn and from all his colleagues. Particular thanks are due to Martin Cahill, Charles Carroll, David Fassbender and Denis O'Connell, who provided valuable reminiscences. I also owe a particular debt of gratitude to John Rohan and Mary Doyle, whose commitment to the project was such that they were always ready to help me with useful information, research and comments. Many others in the organisation added to my store of knowledge. Kay Barry, Donal Brick, Clare Connellan, Tony Davis, Emma Harrington, Bernadette Hudson, Eamon Keogh, Ken McEvoy, Pauline McLaughlin, Noel MacMahon, Rosaleen McManus, John O'Neill, Roisin Quigley, John Staunton, Frank Treanor and Martin Thornton were most generous in the help they gave me. Relevant archives were unearthed for me by Jan Power.

I am also grateful to some former colleagues in ICC for their assistance. Louis Heelan and Jack Ryan, two people with whom I worked very closely during my time in ICC, deserve a particular expression of appreciation but there were many others, notably Tony Cody, Leo Conway, Colum Kelleher, Kevin McGuinness, Kevin O'Connell, Pat O'Reilly, Seamus O'Shea, Gerry Tierney and Larry Tuomey.

I must pay a special tribute to Professor Dermot McAleese, who kindly read an early draft and made comments and suggestions which were very helpful to me when I set about revising the text.

The list of those outside ICC who helped me would fill another book if I mentioned everyone. I would like, however, to express particular gratitude to Tony Barry, Des Byrne, James Cawley, John Donnelly, Kieran Flynn, Kerry Holland, Cyril McGuire, Eugene McCague, Hugh Mackeown, Brian Matthews, Carmel Motherway, Michael Murphy, Joe Murray, Eugene Murtagh, Seamus O'Carroll, Ken Rohan, Charles Sinnott, Dr T. K. Whitaker and Judith Woodworth. Those mentioned provided assistance either by offering personal reminiscences or useful books of reference. I would like to refer in particular to Mrs Terry Kirwan, a daughter of the late Dr J.P. Beddy, who very kindly allowed me to see some relevant papers and photographs from her father's collection. Special thanks are also due to Colm Donlon of IDA-Ireland and Aisling Nic an tShithigh of Enterprise Ireland, who provided me with much useful material and information.

I am very grateful to Joan Barnewell and Angela Healy who speedily and efficiently converted my dictated musings into something more readily comprehensible. I would also like to thank James Norman who kindly suggested the title for the book. I reserve my final words of appreciation for my wife Alison and my daughters, Philippa and Jane, who gave me generous help and advice and did not complain about the domestic inconvenience of having an author at work about the house for the best part of a year.

The story of a bank does not always make for very exciting reading. My fear that the book would become too turgid caused me to leaven the text with occasional light-hearted reminiscences. I hope that in the process I have not in any way trivialised the story of an organisation for which I have long-standing admiration and affection.

Frank Casey
August 2000

Prologue

The Irish newspapers of 5 July 1933 reported that Dublin Port was crippled by a strike and that efforts to solve it were not meeting with immediate success. This gloomy economic news was supplemented by a report that shipping and the shipbuilding industry worldwide were in poor shape. Ireland was enjoying or enduring a heat wave and it was unfortunately accompanied by a series of accidents and fatalities. Although the Irish Free State had been in existence for more than a decade, the social and personal columns devoted considerable attention to the engagements of the British monarch and the Prince of Wales. The diligent reader would have had to search the inside pages for a report of the Dáil debate on the Industrial Credit Bill which provided for the establishment of The Industrial Credit Company, Limited, which is now ICC Bank plc.

The then Minister for Finance, Seán MacEntee, did his best to make the subject interesting, but there is no evidence that a lively debate ensued. Probably the most amusing, if somewhat uninformed, comment came from a backbencher who was unimpressed by the proposed legislation. He suggested that, if the company envisaged in the Bill were the subject of a public flotation, the relevant document inviting share subscriptions would be denounced as a bucket-shop prospectus. In a more serious vein, it is worth noting that the minister said: 'It is the desire of the government that ultimately the control of this company should be taken over by the Irish investing public'. During the debate, doubts, couched in less colourful language than those already mentioned, were expressed as to the viability of the proposed company. The minister did his best to respond positively to the fears expressed. The Bill passed all its stages by the end of July 1933.

With little more than a whimper, the Industrial Credit Company, Limited (ICC) came into existence on 4 October

1

1933. It made an issue of £500,000 share capital in November 1933. While the government was anxious to make ownership of ICC available to the Irish public, it recognised that the issue would probably not be well subscribed and consequently underwrote it. The Irish public, failing to perceive that this new corporate baby was destined to have a bright future, took up 7,936 shares (1.6 per cent) and the minister subscribed for the remaining 492,064 shares (98.4 per cent). ICC thus became not only a state-sponsored, but also a state-controlled, body – and one with the unique distinction, among such bodies, of having its shares quoted on the stock exchange.

1

The Economic and Social Background

In the decade leading up to the establishment of ICC, the Irish Free State had encountered many difficulties, starting with the Civil War and culminating in the Great Depression which followed the Wall Street crash of 1929. When the state was founded in 1921, Ireland was primarily an agricultural country. Practically all manufactured goods were imported, mostly from Great Britain. British manufacturers enjoyed many advantages in supplying Ireland. There were no language difficulties; consumer tastes were very similar; there was no currency risk; and the circulation of many British newspapers in Ireland meant that British goods were widely advertised here. These advantages, except those relating to currency, still exist today. The first Irish government introduced a measure of protection for indigenous industry, but basically the new state was a free trade country which derived most of its income from abroad by exporting live animals and agricultural produce to Great Britain.

In 1923 the Shannon Scheme, whereby water power would be used to generate electricity, was proposed. By 1927 all necessary studies had been concluded and the Shannon Scheme commenced. This was the start of rural electrification and was a major step towards the establishment of the Electricity Supply Board. In the same year the Agricultural Credit Corporation (now ACCBank) came into existence, and the setting up of a sugar manufacturing plant in Carlow made possible for the first time in Ireland the production of sugar from sugar beet. Apart from these major new enterprises, the main Irish industries were brewing, distilling and biscuit-making.

To add to the young state's difficulties, the Great Depression in the early 1930s caused a huge increase in unemployment. The Fianna Fáil government, elected in 1932, pursued an economic policy based on switching the emphasis in agriculture from livestock to tillage, and also building up the manufacturing sector. Heavy tariffs and quotas were imposed on imports. The Control of Manufactures Acts of 1932 and 1934 required that more than half the total capital and at least two thirds of the voting shares in Irish companies should be in the beneficial ownership of Irish nationals. There was also a requirement that a majority of the directors should be Irish. The control restrictions were often more honoured in the breach than in the observance. With the assistance of able lawyers, foreign companies were able to achieve virtually total control by having a very small number of voting shares and placing a majority of these in friendly Irish hands.

Life became more complicated as a result of the economic war with Great Britain. This war was caused by the decision of the new government to discontinue the payment of annuities to that country. The British government imposed retaliatory tariffs and quotas on imports of agricultural produce from Ireland. The economic war did not end until the Anglo-Irish Agreement of 1938, when the Irish government made a single payment of £10 million and the British government cancelled the annuities.

It is not surprising that economic difficulties were accompanied by social deprivation. Poverty, never too far away, even in buoyant economic times, was widespread in the 1930s. The unemployment caused by the Great Depression and the economic war added to the general misery, particularly as the social services at that time were much less generous than they are today. Barefooted children could frequently be seen throughout Ireland. Life in town and country was dispiriting. The safety valve of employment in Great Britain, which was to be so welcome to the Irish during and after World War 2, was not readily available at a time when unemployment in Great Britain was also high. In all, the 1930s were dismal years in Ireland and elsewhere. One of the most popular American songs during those years was the self-explanatory 'Brother, Can You Spare a Dime?' When one is tempted to criticise the protected industries which grew up in that period, it should be remembered that, without the level of employment which they provided, the social and economic situation in the Ireland of the 1930s would have been far worse.

So much of what we take for granted at the beginning of the twenty-first century did not exist in the early 1930s. Motor transport was limited; much more common sights were the brewery dray horse, the horse-drawn bread van and the milk cart. Funeral hearses were drawn by black-plumed horses. There were many cinemas, though 'talkies' were a very recent innovation. Radio existed, but radio sets were expensive and not widely owned. On the day of an All-Ireland final, practically all the residents of a street would visit the only house which possessed a radio set to hear the live commentary. Television had been recently invented, but it only became commercially feasible in the late 1930s and, having been interrupted by World War 2, did not flourish until many years later. There were gramophone records, but long-playing records (LPs) had not yet been invented, and anyone who prophesied the development of audio and video-cassettes, compact discs and DVDs would have been regarded as an amiable eccentric. The telephone system was quite unlike its modern counterpart – all calls were mediated by an operator, and there were no mobile phones, no faxes, no e-mail. The friendly local grocer was still pre-eminent; the age of the supermarket had not yet arrived. Computers had not even been dreamed of by ordinary mortals. Simple calculating machines were expensive and unwieldy and mental arithmetic was still a much-favoured and much-used skill.

It was against this political, economic, social and technological background that ICC came into existence. If Irish industry was to grow, a more extensive level of financial support than that offered at the time by the commercial banks would be needed.

2

With Shining Morning Face

In preparing legislation for the establishment of ICC, the government had in mind the circumstances which had led to the early demise of its predecessor, the Industrial Trust Company (ITC). That ill-fated company was set up in 1925 with an initial capital of £100,000, of which half was contributed by the Irish government. Although the capital was later increased to £163,000 by means of subscriptions by shareholders in the United States, ITC failed to prosper. In a virtually free trade environment, few entrepreneurs were encouraged to set up industrial concerns and hence there were not many approaches to ITC. Such applications as were made were usually declined unless a government guarantee was forthcoming. ITC invested much of its capital abroad and, having taken a financial bath as a result of the Wall Street crisis, it went into receivership in 1933.

In 1932 John P. Colbert, then chairman of the Agricultural Credit Corporation (ACC), submitted to government a memorandum proposing that ACC should have its powers extended to enable it to finance industry as well as agriculture. The specific proposal did not find favour with the government, particularly with Seán Lemass, then Minister for Industry and Commerce. However, it led to the decision to create a specialist body – ICC – for the financing of industry. At that time the commercial banks, not only in Ireland, but in most countries, did not provide long-term finance for capital requirements and limited their participation to overdrafts for working capital. Pursuant to the Industrial Credit Act of 1933, ICC would be empowered to provide long-term capital by way of loans, share capital investment and the underwriting of public flotations. Opposition deputies were concerned about the risks involved. However, they recognised the need for a new institution of the kind proposed and did not vote against the Bill. And so, ICC was born. Its only competitor in Ireland, Guinness Mahon & Company (now part of Irish Life and Permanent), had been set up ninety-seven years earlier by Robert Rundell Guinness and John Ross Mahon in a four-storey house in South Frederick Street, Dublin. The lighting in their office was initially by oil lamps and candles and the partners travelled to and from work by jaunting car. I describe in chapter 3 the less romantic setting in which ICC was to begin its activities.

The first chairman and managing director of ICC was John P. Colbert, who had been chairman of ACC since its establishment in 1927. He had been a colleague of J. J. McElligott, secretary of the Department of Finance, when they were both journalists in London in the early 1920s. His City background was of great value to ICC, particularly during its early years when the main activity was underwriting public issues by new and established concerns.

At the time ICC was established, there were only twenty-four industrial companies quoted on the Irish Stock Exchange, with a combined market value of about £5 million (approximately £215 million in today's terms). To put this in perspective, the market capitalisation of companies listed on the Irish Stock Exchange at the end of 1999 was almost £56 billion. Only one public issue, for a mere £15,000, had taken place between 1922 and 1930. Between 1934 and 1938 ICC sponsored twenty-seven new issues which raised nearly £5 million. Thus, the number and value of the quoted shares of companies listed on the Irish Stock Exchange approximately doubled as a result of ICC's early underwriting and issuing house activities. Reference is made later to some of the companies whose shares were brought to the market by ICC during the 1930s.

Today a company intending to have a public flotation of its shares has to meet the very rigorous requirements of the Irish

Stock Exchange. All relevant details must be disclosed and, where possible, corroborated by reports from independent experts. While the Irish Stock Exchange had stringent requirements in the 1930s, the appetite for detail was less developed than it is today and the essential part of any prospectus occupied less than two (admittedly large and unwieldy) pages. Apart from Guinness Mahon & Company which, in accordance with best City of London practice, sponsored flotations only for established companies, there was no other Irish issuing house at that time. ICC, with all the enthusiasm of youth, launched a series of prospectuses which in some cases amounted to an appeal to the Irish investing public to make an act of faith in what were little more than green fields and heady aspirations for the future. The relative success of these flotations was, in part, due to a provision in the Finance Act of 1932, whereby individuals subscribing for stocks and shares in public companies could obtain an abatement of 20 per cent on the tax payable on interest or dividends on those stocks or shares.

Even though the prospectuses of the 1930s were by today's standards unsophisticated, a great deal of care went into their preparation. All statements of fact were checked and double-checked. The words used were subjected to intense scrutiny and no infelicitous phrase was wittingly allowed to defile the text. Even a capital letter or a comma in the wrong place would be a sufficient reason to send the draft prospectus back to the printer for re-proofing. The care lavished on the prospectus did not end when the pages had been finalised. Technology in those days was not as advanced as it is today and, as it was the practice to publish the complete prospectus in each of the national daily newspapers, it was necessary to check the newspaper proofs against the original prospectus. Since some of the material, particularly routine items like articles of association, was in very small print, the checking of the newspaper proofs could only be accomplished with the help of a magnifying glass. All this effort would be regarded as justified if, as was usually the case, an error was found. ICC's advertising agents, who were supposed to have checked the proofs independently, would then be strongly criticised for their failure to attend to detail and warned that a repetition of this dereliction of duty might lead to their replacement by another practitioner with a keener and more reliable eye.

It is easy to scoff at some of these early issues, particularly those which were for companies that subsequently failed. However, it must be remembered that the flotations were often for brand-new industries trying to make their way in a hostile environment where there was no tradition of industrial skill and limited commercial expertise. The economic war with Great Britain was in full swing and, while the home market was protected, there was a belief among consumers that the quality of the domestic product was inferior to that of the imported article. This belief was sometimes correct, but often it sprang from prejudice. For example, one woman complained that, following the establishment of the Irish Sugar Company, the lump sugar she bought did not adequately sweeten her coffee. As the Irish Sugar Company did not at that time produce lump sugar, her criticism was misdirected.

The first board and management of ICC deserve plaudits for their courage in bringing to the market companies which had many difficulties to contend with in Ireland where the development of an industrial base was no easy task. Although the early ICC might seem like a corporate Don Quixote, undertaking heroic deeds against impossible odds, it had a good track record. It is interesting to look back at some of the companies which ICC sponsored in the 1930s.

The first issue was for Ranks (Ireland) Limited in March 1934 and was underwritten jointly by ICC and one of its stock-brokers, Butler & Briscoe. Only two weeks later the second issue, for the Irish Sugar Company, was launched. Before the end of the year ICC had underwritten four more issues – for Arklow Pottery, Irish Tanners of Portlaw, Irish Aluminium Company of Nenagh, and a second issue for the Irish Sugar Company. From this snapshot of the first year's operations, some interesting points emerge. Firstly, the carrying out of six public flotations in a nine-month period was in itself a major achievement. Secondly, the locations of the companies brought to the market represented a considerable geographical spread. Thirdly, the issues showed that the young Irish economy was getting to grips with new and diverse industries. For example, Irish Tanners produced leather for the emerging footwear industry and Irish Aluminium brought to the market the 'Castle' brand of aluminium ware, which is still deservedly popular today.

The year 1935 was even more active, with nine issues taking place between February and the end of the year. Some of these were for companies which no longer exist. However, it is satisfying to reflect that as long ago as 1935 two of today's successful companies – Newbridge Cutlery Company and Irish Wire Products (now part of IWP) – were introduced to the market.

In the next 3½ years preceding World War 2, ICC sponsored fourteen more issues. Some of these issues were for textile companies like General Textiles Limited, Salts Ireland Limited and Irish Worsted Mills Limited, which have since been wound up but which provided valuable employment at that time in Athlone, Tullamore and Portlaoise. These new companies also created in those towns a climate that was receptive to the establishment of new industries and a workforce that became accustomed to the disciplines and procedures of life in an industrial production unit. It would be unfair to criticise the ICC of the 1930s for launching on the market footwear and textile industries which were later to cease operations. It is a feature of emerging nations that the first units in an industrialisation programme tend to be low in technology. This very fact undoubtedly led in due course to the demise of some of those Irish companies which were unable to withstand competition from low-cost developing countries.

Not all of the failures can be attributed to external factors. When one textile company, which produced cloth for suiting, ran into difficult times, its unenterprising management, instead of thinking of diversification, attributed its difficulties to the unforgivable decision of young Irishmen to abandon waistcoats. A headwear manufacturer, faced with diminishing turnover, wrung his hands and complained, 'Why won't they wear hats any more?'

In those early days of industrial development, the concept of 'conflict of interest' was not always treated with the same reverence as today. When an industry was being established, it was not unusual to find that the promoting group included a representative of the distributive trade engaged in the sale of imported products similar to those which would be made by the new indigenous industry. Such experience and expertise were valuable, but sometimes the distributor concerned would join the board of the new Irish company and some undesirable practices developed. For example, ICC found on one occasion that most of the output of a manufacturing concern was being sold through a wholesale agency owned or controlled by one of the directors. Internal records show that, where ICC became aware of such practices, it took immediate and decisive steps to have the offending director removed.

That ICC took its responsibilities to the investing public seriously is emphasised by the following excerpt from the statement made by Colbert as chairman to the first annual general meeting of ICC:

> The investor can best safeguard himself against issues of an undesirable character by confining himself to those which are sponsored by issuing houses with a standing and reputation to maintain. In this matter, The Industrial Credit Company takes a broader view of its responsibilities than is usual with issuing houses which are run purely for the making of profits. Not only does it occupy naturally a position of leadership in this field, but it has also a certain national responsibility in seeing that any new projects which come before it are planned on the soundest possible lines technically, commercially and financially. Every underwriting proposition that comes before us is examined with the greatest care and is not presented to the public until we are perfectly satisfied that it represents a reasonable industrial risk.

The issuing house activity was carried out with a tiny staff. Because ICC handled all the paperwork in public issues, and was proud of doing so, it was necessary to augment the staff temporarily whenever application forms had to be processed and letters of allotment issued. The usual source of outside assistance was the Faculty of Commerce in University College, Dublin (UCD), where impecunious students were only too pleased to have the opportunity of earning some money (as an alternative or supplement to pawning their overcoats or selling their text books). UCD may have been chosen because ICC's chairman and secretary were both part-time lecturers in the college's Faculty of Commerce. ICC might seem to have been taking a huge risk by entrusting such demanding work to students. However, ICC's concern with accuracy and thoroughness led to a meticulous checking of the students' work.

As I did not join ICC until 1947, I was not involved in any of the pre-war public issues. My time in UCD coincided with the war years when there was little activity in the financial world. I have, however, a clear recollection of how issues were processed. My first days in ICC coincided with one such flotation. There was a feverish excitement in the air. Application forms were classified, allotment letters were prepared, cheques were written for amounts overpaid, and all this work was carefully checked before anything was posted to applicants. From top management down, everyone was expected to cast aside all other work and deal with these arduous but intellectually unchallenging tasks. On one occasion a member of staff had to be rushed to hospital because he had damaged his hand while trying to rescue someone from a lift that had come to an unexpected halt between floors. Concern was expressed, less for his plight than for the possibility that his absence might lead to a serious disruption of the workflow.

Because Colbert had been 'brought up' in the City of London, he had a knowledge of City practices in the matter of public flotations. At least one of his obiter dicta would bring a smile to the faces of most of today's practitioners in this area. According to him, if a flotation proposal was brought to a potential underwriter, the proposer would be asked whether participation had been offered to anyone else.

If it transpired that this was the case, the proposal would be rejected out of hand. In similar circumstances today, a more likely question would be whether there was anyone to whom the business had not been offered.

Colbert had an almost irrational objection to the acceptance by ICC of sub-underwriting, whereby the main underwriter spread some or all of the risk among other financial institutions. He seemed to feel that in some way the dignity of ICC would be tarnished if it adopted a junior role in someone else's flotation. On the other hand, ICC itself was a particularly generous dispenser of sub-underwriting, so much so that, if there was an underwriting liability, the sub-underwriters would often receive commission without being asked to take up their liability. The motivation for this generosity appears to have been a desire to keep the stockbrokers, who were the main sub-underwriters, in good spirits, ensuring their continuing support for ICC issues and avoiding any risk that they would upset the market by a hurried sale of shares acquired as a result of sub-underwriting. Whether these objectives were achieved or not is a matter for conjecture. One cannot help feeling that a sub-underwriter who knew that his liability would be nil would have less incentive to work diligently for the success of an issue than if he were aware that he might be called upon to put up money.

ICC's other main activity in the initial years was the provision of long-term loans to industry. ICC had limited capital resources and the Department of Finance, which had not welcomed the establishment of ICC, was reluctant to provide it with any more money. In its first three years ICC's total lending amounted to little more than £300,000 (about £13 million in today's terms). This was in sharp contrast to ICC's public issue activity which was responsible for raising more than £4 million (more than £160 million in current terms) in the same period.

In those days every loan application, however small, had to be submitted to the board of ICC. Detailed reports on these proposals were prepared but, however keen management was on a particular proposal, the directors would discover a fatal flaw. The company records indicate that the members of the board, although decisive in many other respects, were like cats with a mouse when dealing with these early loan proposals. Having discussed the flaw, they would attempt to make the proposal more acceptable by drawing the applicant's attention to the weakness in the hope that it would be rectified. Unhappily, the revised proposition would almost inevitably give rise to some new considerations which would necessitate further discussions with the applicant.

It is not too surprising that there was so much difficulty in reaching decisions on loan applications. Many of those who submitted proposals were new to business and were hoping to prosper in a less than friendly environment. Sometimes they had very little capital of their own to contribute. Besides, it is well known that when a new financial institution is set up, practically every dubious entrepreneur in the country makes an application to it. Under the legislation setting up ICC, no loan could be advanced without security. However, although security was the key to the door, proposals were not accepted if it was felt that there was a real possibility that security would have to be enforced.

Borrowers were not expected to have about them the odour of sanctity, but there was a deep suspicion of those who indulged in vices like excessive drinking or gambling. The feeling was that, if they couldn't control their personal lives, they were unlikely to be able to manage their businesses effectively. An extreme example was that of a borrower who, on being found to have wagered a considerable sum of money at Cheltenham, was urged to repay his ICC loan without delay. The loan was repaid and the former borrower, who is understood to have gambled more than £1 million during his lifetime, continued to be a familiar figure at racecourses, where he enjoyed considerable success without doing any apparent damage to his very prosperous business.

3

A Team of All the Talents

The Industrial Credit Act of 1933 provided that the managing director and half of the non-executive directors would be nominated by the Minister for Finance and that the other half of the non-executive directors would be elected by the shareholders. As the bulk of the shares have remained in the hands of the Minister for Finance, the minister has in practice appointed all directors of ICC. During ICC's first three decades, the board changed very little, but in later years, with more frequent changes of government, new appointments have become more numerous.

Because the first board was breaking new ground and involved itself so much in the day-to-day affairs of the company, it may be useful to look back at those early board members and the qualities which may have led to their appointment by the government.

The first chairman and managing director, J. P. Colbert, was a commerce graduate of University College, Cork. He spent the early part of the 1920s in London as a financial journalist, eventually becoming editor of *The Statist*, which was then one of the leading British financial journals. When the Agricultural Credit Corporation was founded, Colbert returned to Ireland to become its chairman. He and his abilities were, of course, well known to the then secretary of the Department of Finance, J. J. McElligott, who had preceded Colbert as editor of *The Statist*. When ICC was established, Colbert was asked to transfer to it. Although he was anything but a typical banker, he must take much of the

15

credit for the innovative role which ICC played, particularly in the 1930s.

Colbert had a great interest in the arts and was friendly with many who shared that interest. Outside office hours he would meet with literary giants and journalists in well-known Dublin bars, notably the Palace Bar off Westmoreland Street. Colbert's associates in these hostelries and in the United Arts Club included such renowned figures as Oliver St John Gogarty, Brian O'Nolan (Myles na gCopaleen) and R. M. Smyllie (editor of *The Irish Times*).

Although Colbert scrupulously kept his business and private lives separate, there were occasions when there was a hint of an overlap. One of these was the aftermath of a visit by him to a small industrial enterprise outside the city of Dublin. When the visit had been concluded, the proprietor, knowing that Colbert had artistic leanings, invited him to his home where refreshments were provided and the proprietor's teenage daughter played some piano music for Colbert's benefit. So moved was Colbert by the performance that his eyes became tear-dimmed. He grasped the industrialist by the hand and told him that his daughter had played divinely and had wonderful prospects as a musician. The proprietor interpreted this expression of admiration for his off-spring as an indication that his company's application for a loan would be favourably received. However, by the following day the critical faculties of Colbert the businessman had reasserted themselves and, although the sound of great music was still ringing in his ears, he did not consider the project a worthy one for ICC participation.

J. J. O'Leary remained on the board of ICC for thirty-nine years and thereby set a record for ICC board membership. He was also a founding director of Aer Lingus and a member of the board of that company for thirty-six years. A self-made businessman, he owned and controlled Cahill & Company Limited, printers. Although he would not have claimed to be an intellectual, he was very interested in the arts and numbered many famous musicians and actors among his friends. He was also a very keen yachtsman. In business, he had an astute mind and could sense rather than analyse the quality of a business proposition. His favourite phrase was 'pound for pound', meaning that, in his view, ICC should do no more than match the amount put up by the applicant. This relatively unsophisticated formula did not always commend itself to his colleagues on the board.

Dr L. J. Kettle, who was a brother of the late Tom Kettle (a member of the Irish Parliamentary Party and a professor of national economics in UCD, who was killed in France during World War 1), was an engineer by profession. He had been involved in the Shannon Scheme and was appointed to the board of the Electricity Supply Board. During his twenty-seven years on the ICC board, he was the perfect foil to J. J. O'Leary, being a shy and taciturn man. He was slow to express an opinion, even though that opinion had been reached carefully and methodically, unless he felt that the view he expressed would help his colleagues to arrive at a decision.

Tim Caffrey was an accountant who became managing director of the National City Bank (subsequently taken over by Bank of Ireland). Like most bankers of his time, he was conservative and may well have influenced the mood of the original ICC board when it considered loan applications. His period of office lasted for sixteen years until his death in 1949.

The fourth non-executive director was John F. Punch, managing director of the shoe polish manufacturing concern of the same name. Lugubrious in appearance and conservative in business matters, he astounded his colleagues when they found that he was an automobile fanatic who regularly drove from Cork to Dublin in open-top cars of his own construction. His period of office lasted for ten years until he was appointed a director of the Central Bank.

Although M. W. O'Reilly was not a founder director, he was appointed in 1943 when John Punch retired and he was to remain on the ICC board for twenty-nine years. His presence on the board for so many of ICC's early years makes it possible to speak of him as if he were part of the original board. He was chairman and managing director of New

Ireland Assurance Company and had many other business interests. He had a strong sense of national pride and was well suited to an organisation like ICC. He was autocratic in manner and firm in his judgements. He reserved his strongest criticisms for applicant companies which had allowed the level of creditors to exceed prudent limits.

The board enjoyed the services of J. P. Beddy, the first company secretary of ICC, who was later to become chairman and managing director and played a major part in the development of the company. As company secretary, he had a very considerable influence on progress and policies in the 1930s and 1940s. He had been an inspector of taxes and brought to his task in ICC an enquiring mind which caused him to look critically at virtually every statement made to him by those who sought ICC's financial support.

To a reader today, the minutes of early ICC board meetings have an unusual flavour, although one gathers that their deliberations were not out of line with the procedures adopted in other companies at that time. Nothing was too unimportant to be submitted to the board, and trivia occupied some of the time of what was then a weekly meeting, although the records show that directors found it possible to take time off in Christmas week. So, despite all the effort expended by them in assessing loan and underwriting propositions, they nevertheless managed to find time to consider such earth-shattering matters as the weekly wages of the office messenger and the purchase of a small item of office equipment. Even a shareholder's dividend mandate had to be considered by the board before it was accepted. Despite their heavy workload, they did not welcome any opportunity to lighten it. At an early board meeting, the chairman tried to encourage them to delegate to a committee the processing of loan applications for amounts not exceeding £500. The board decided not to embrace this opportunity to ease their burden.

One thing that did not concern the first board was any excessive expenditure on office premises. The original premises at 9 Leinster Street in Dublin was a modest set of offices, rented at £150 per annum, plus rates. It was located over a shop and café operated by Johnston, Mooney & O'Brien, the bakery company. The café was the nearest ICC personnel could get in those days to a staff restaurant. Its main attraction was proximity. Depending on the size of one's purse, a limited amount of choice was available. The wealthier staff were able to afford such staple foods as bacon, egg and sausage (8p in decimal currency) or, on special occasions, a venture into items of haute cuisine like grilled ham and chips (10p). Lesser mortals had to content themselves with modest repasts like beans on toast (4p) or, on extremely impecunious days, peas on toast (3p). If one ventured into the café for morning coffee (1p), it was necessary to share the available space with hordes of students from the Dental Hospital in nearby Lincoln Place.

If the board were unconcerned about the lack of staff canteen facilities, they were not themselves interested in being fed and watered. On one of the rare occasions that they had lunch together, they adjourned to a leading Dublin hotel and were handed a menu which might have been designed to test their knowledge of French. Undaunted, one director astounded the restaurant staff by spurning the culinary delights offered to him and insisting that his own favourite food, tinned salmon, be provided. It may well have been the resultant loss of face that discouraged the board from having more frequent festive occasions together.

The offices were extremely spartan. The chairman and company secretary enjoyed the luxury of a carpet, but the rest of the office floors were either bare boards or covered in cheap linoleum. The second-hand furniture and absence of curtains fitted in with the general impression of drabness. Even the waiting room was uninviting. It must be remembered that during those times there would undoubtedly have been criticism of anything suggestive of luxurious living. The offices were probably no different in character to those occupied by the civil service at that time. Dr C. S. Andrews wrote: 'Rooms in Civil Service offices to which the public had access were notoriously untidy and ill-equipped and the state of the lavatories was deplorable' (Andrews, 1982: p. 67). C. H. Murray, former secretary of the

Department of Finance, was equally hard-hitting: 'In the past, the standard of civil service accommodation was often disgraceful and frequently in breach of the Offices Acts. It took a combination of trade union pressure and the need to improve public reception areas to effect much needed changes' (Murray, 1990: pp. 152–3).

The only concession to luxury in ICC was an internal rule (which, surprisingly, does not seem to have required board sanction) allowing executives to travel first-class by train when visiting the premises of customers or potential customers. This concession did not lead to riotous extravagance on the part of ICC executives who did not own cars. They often found themselves travelling on a CIÉ bus to visit customers in the Dublin area. It can safely be said that ICC's profits in its early years were not adversely affected by excessive administrative expenditure.

The concern to keep operating expenses to a minimum was reflected in the numbers and remuneration of staff. During the 1930s ICC had a total staff of ten, including the managing director, the company secretary, the accountant, the assistant accountant and one young executive. Their number was reduced to nine in 1936 when that executive, Richard Cooke, left to study law; he subsequently became an eminent senior counsel and 'Father of the Bar'. Eleven years were to pass before he was replaced in ICC. When staff were appointed in the 1930s, their modest salaries were 'subject to such increase as the board may be pleased to grant in the course of time'. The jobs market in the 1930s was a good deal less buoyant than it is today.

4

ICC and the Banking Commission

When things are not going well for politicians, they sometimes introduce a diversionary tactic. Whether the 1934 government was so motivated or not, one of its actions was to set up a Banking Commission which reported in 1938. The chairman was Joseph Brennan, the former secretary of the Department of Finance and chairman of the Currency Commission, and the members included J. J. McElligott, secretary of the Department of Finance, and several leading national and international economists. One of these was Professor George O'Brien of University College, Dublin. For years afterwards, O'Brien spoke to his students reverently about the majority report of the Commission, even going so far as to compare the report to a Wagnerian opera, full, as he put it, of delightful and recurring motifs. The report served as a good textbook, but, notwithstanding O'Brien's satisfaction with it, there were a number of dissident voices on the Commission, and no fewer than three minority reports, and some reservations, were written. This is not the place to go into the main recommendations of the Commission, except to mention that it proposed the establishment of a Central Bank; in general, its attitude was that there should be little change and that such changes as were made should be repressive rather than expansionist.

The chairman of ICC, J. P. Colbert, was a member of the Commission and was understandably not impressed by a section of the report which sought to limit ICC's activities. The report said:

The scope for future activity in this sphere [underwriting] is likely to be much more limited than heretofore, as the more obvious openings have already been filled and the rate of fresh demands for capital may be expected to fall off, so that such demands as may arise should be met with less difficulty. This should facilitate a curtailment of the activities of the Company in this field, a development which we think desirable. (Department of Finance, 1938: p.273)

The report recommended that ICC's loan business might ultimately be discharged by a merger with the ACC. It recommended that, in the meantime, the issued share capital of ICC should not exceed £1 million, that its borrowing powers should be very severely curtailed, that the maximum loan to any borrower should not exceed £10,000, and that the sanction of the Minister for Finance should be required in each case involving a remission of bad loans.

Colbert, in his reservation, pointed out that, 'There is not a particle of evidence put before the Commission which would justify the recommendation that the Oireachtas should, within so brief a period, alter its decision to the point of stultification.' He strongly criticised the recommendation that ICC's underwriting activities be curtailed, describing these suggestions as 'entirely putative and not based on any evidence put before the Commission – and at variance with the available data'. Fortunately for ICC, the Commission's recommendations in regard to the ICC were not adopted and the outcome was not the Wagnerian 'twilight of the gods' that Professor O'Brien, and others who supported the majority report, might have anticipated.

5

War - and Peace

The Irish state was neutral during World War 2 and emphasised its neutrality by designating that period of universal horror as the 'Emergency'. It is generally accepted that the war years were a period of economic stagnation and of considerable deprivation as a result of fuel and other shortages, which led to the rationing of many items, such as tea, butter and sugar. These were items which, particularly at that time, formed a major part of the population's daily diet. The only market that flourished was the black market.

Because coal was scarce, gas, the main source of fuel for domestic cooking, was severely curtailed. It was a serious offence to use gas outside certain specified hours and, for that purpose, inspectors known colloquially as 'Glimmer Men' were employed to seek out and arrange for the punishment of offenders. For heating, the country had to turn to its native turf, some of which was so damp as to be almost unusable. The turf was stored in unusual places; in Dublin, the beautiful green vistas of the Phoenix Park were disrupted by mini-mountains of the dark brown native fuel. An attempt was made to have turf used to power the trains and the resultant time taken to complete a journey would make railway users of today blink in disbelief. It was, for instance, quite usual for a journey from Dublin to Cork to take ten hours in conditions of acute discomfort.

Industrial development became a thing of the past. Factories could not readily acquire new machinery and, even when they could, they had limited raw materials on which to work. Transport limitations added to the difficulties experienced by indigenous industries. Some of the economic hardships were masked by ready access to Northern Ireland and Great Britain, where there was an abundance of jobs because these areas were on a war footing.

If there was not much happening on the industrial scene and if people had to endure all kinds of privation, the politicians and civil servants, faced with such an unfamiliar set of circumstances, found themselves running around in circles. The solution to every wartime problem appears to have been to set up a committee. Probably the first of these was The Civil Service Economy Committee, headed by the parliamentary secretary (junior minister) attached to the Department of Finance. Its brief was self-explanatory. Other committees included an inter-departmental committee on Emergency measures, a cabinet committee on Emergency problems, a committee on Emergency production and a cabinet committee on economic planning.

Two major Emergency Power Orders were made in 1941 with a view to curtailing inflation. One imposed a wage freeze and the other restricted dividend payments. A Reference Tribunal was set up to monitor dividend limitation and it is worth noting that ICC's secretary, J. P. Beddy, was invited to be a member of that three-person tribunal.

While the talking and planning were proceeding, Seán Lemass, who had taken on the role of minister in the new Department of Supplies, seems to have been one of the few members of government who tried to play a proactive role. At the beginning of the war he proposed a number of measures, including the granting of additional powers to ICC to promote and finance industrial development. His proposals were met with something less than wild enthusiasm and, accordingly, ICC was not encouraged to pursue an expansionist course. One of the Lemass initiatives which was of benefit to the country during the war and for many years afterwards was the establishment of Irish Shipping Limited in 1941. By possessing its own cargo ships, the state was able to limit the difficulties involved in obtaining supplies of essential goods and materials from abroad. It is somewhat ironic that the company that did so much for the country in a period of dire need should have been the first state-sponsored body to be wound up, in 1984. By that time it had run into serious financial difficulties and its debts were so monumental that no other course of action was considered possible.

It was naturally impossible for a finance house like ICC to continue with the spate of public flotations which had marked its first six years. During the war years it sponsored only one flotation – for Williams and Woods Limited, now part of Nestlé – in December 1940, raising a total of £196,000. Because of the wartime difficulties experienced by manufacturers who might otherwise have wished to expand, the demand for loans was virtually non-existent. The small staff at ICC spent the war years looking after their limited portfolio of investments and loans. Some of them improved their minds by studying for higher degrees. It was during this period that Beddy completed and published a thesis entitled *'Profits – Theoretical and Practical Aspects'*, for which he was awarded a Doctorate of Economic Science by the National University of Ireland (NUI). Although his significant contribution to the Irish economy was later recognised when he was awarded an Honorary Doctorate of Laws by The University of Dublin (Trinity College), he was always justifiably proud of the fact that his original doctorate had been earned with blood, sweat and tears. He was visibly incensed whenever he was asked why and when the NUI had 'given' him his degree and would reply icily, 'They didn't GIVE it to me; I worked for it'.

Beddy was always impeccably dressed and never ventured into the great outdoors without wearing an elegant trilby hat. Students at University College, Dublin (UCD) during the war years noted that, even though government restrictions made it impossible for Beddy to use his car, the fact that he had to travel to UCD on a bicycle did not cause him to abandon his high sartorial standards. ICC's chairman, Colbert, also lectured at UCD. I recall that, on one occasion, Colbert sternly rebuked a young nun for her failure to attend several of his lectures on banking and finance. A commerce student at the back of the lecture theatre begged him facetiously (but successfully) to spare her blushes. The student who came to the nun's rescue was none other than a future Taoiseach Charles J. Haughey.

The war years cannot have been an enjoyable or morale-boosting period for the ICC staff. However, an organisation that had started life so energetically in the pre-war years may have needed a pause so that it could prepare itself for the post-war world. Following the period of relative inactivity, there was a short period of expansion in the years immediately after the war. Regrettably, this expansion was destined to be followed by several years of recession.

6

After the War was Over

The 'Emergency' ended in 1945 and, while rationing was to continue for a considerable time, the economy quickly got back on its feet – a remarkable achievement for a young state that had, in its twenty-three years, experienced a civil war, an economic war and a world war. One of the country's few advantages was that, because it had been neutral in the world war, its infrastructure, such as it was, had not been damaged.

Most of the countries which had been involved in World War 2 were in poor shape when peace came. However, world politicians showed themselves anxious to set up organisations which would aim to ensure peace and to help needy countries. The Dumbarton Oaks Conference, held in 1944 in a house of the same name in Washington D.C., led to the establishment of the United Nations Organisation in San Francisco in 1945. The International Monetary Fund and the International Bank for Reconstruction and Development (generally known as the World Bank) were also born during this period. Although Ireland was not to join the United Nations until 1955, the establishment of the organisation, despite occasional subsequent hiccoughs, contributed to a better world and, hence, a happier external environment for the Irish state.

At home, there were several political and economic developments during these post-war years. Another Lemass initiative, the Industrial Relations Act of 1946, led to the setting up of the Labour Court, which has since played an important role in the settlement of many industrial disputes.

The 1948 general election had a surprise outcome. Fianna Fáil had been in power since 1932 and emerged as the largest single party, but the other parties between them commanded more Dáil seats and they combined to form a coalition government. At the time, because the term 'coalition' was not generally favoured, they described themselves as an 'inter-party government'.

The new government is usually remembered for declaring the former Irish Free State a republic and for withdrawing from the British Commonwealth. However, it also had other matters to attend to. One of its economic tasks was to obtain loans and grants from the United States government under the Marshall Aid Recovery Programme, which had been introduced by the United States in order to help countries to recover from the effects of World War 2. The monies negotiated from the United States were spent on land rehabilitation and other infrastructural purposes. In order to negotiate these Marshall Aid funds, Ireland had to prepare a planning document. This was entitled *Long Term Recovery Programme* and was published in 1949. Although it was later derided for its grandiose and unrealisable predictions, it was nevertheless the forerunner of the serious planning that was to begin in the succeeding decade.

While all this was happening in the world outside, ICC had shed the somnolent mantle which had been forced upon it during the war years and re-embarked on what was still its main business – the underwriting of public flotations. As there had been only one new issue during the war years, there was an accumulation of funds held by investors and a great deal of pent-up demand. In 1946 there were three successful issues, totalling £507,500. The first ICC-sponsored post-war issue was for the Athlone-based General Textiles in May 1946. In the following month an issue for Irish Ropes Limited, now part of the Barlo Group, was launched. In October of that year there was a successful issue by the Irish Wallboard Company Limited, Athy. However, the post-war issues with the most successful outcome were to occur in the following year.

One of the most heavily over-subscribed post-war flotations was an issue of preference shares by Gypsum Industries

Limited in March 1947. By all accounts, the processing of that issue, which attracted 6,000 applications (then a very high figure), was one of near frenzy. There was only a limited amount of time between the closing of the lists and the sending out of allotment letters. Work went on around the clock but, although complaints about the stressful nature of the work were made by some members of staff, there was a general feeling of satisfaction and, indeed, pride in the successful conclusion of such a major effort.

Within a month of the Gypsum issue, there was an over-subscribed issue by the footwear manufacturer John Rawson & Sons (Ireland) Limited. Soon afterwards a smaller issue was made by Wallpapers Limited, the Kildare plant which made valiant efforts to supply the Irish market but which ultimately failed because of dumping by foreign competitors. The total amount raised by the 1947 flotations was £478,800.

The public issue successes continued in 1948 and 1949, although at nothing like the pre-war pace. There were four issues totalling £347,500 in 1948, two for leather producing companies, one for Greenmount & Boyne Linen Company, and one for Irish Wire Products. By 1949 the bubble was showing signs of bursting, with only two issues (raising £451,000) taking place in that year. One of these issues was for the yarn manufacturer Salts Ireland Limited of Tullamore. This company was very much an offshoot of the UK yarn producer Salts Limited of Saltaire, Yorkshire. More significant, in the context of what would happen later, was the second issue of 1949, which was for a wholly indigenous undertaking, Clondalkin Concrete Limited. Many of the earlier issues had been dependent on foreign participation in the ownership and management of the companies concerned. Here, however, was a business which was owned and for the most part managed by Irish people, mainly the Crampton, Archer and Lyons families, and in which Irish investors were happy to invest.

In the late 1940s and the 1950s some new immigrants arrived in Ireland because of the effects of the war and the subsequent Communist takeover of several central and eastern European countries. Many of these refugees brought with them considerable expertise and valuable business experience. Inevitably, there were a few who misrepresented their past in the hope of achieving a prosperous future for themselves but happily they were a tiny minority.

One of those who has lingered in my memory was a self-styled doctor of engineering from an East European country. This 'doctor' supplemented his natural charm with some amusing observations on the Irish scene. He believed that those whom he described as 'priestmen' were largely responsible for rural inertia. He had observed that Irish country towns did not come to life until the 10 o'clock Mass was concluded. While at the time his criticism might have offended the clergy, the 'priestmen' of today would undoubtedly regard it as a welcome indication of pastoral success.

As a group, the new immigrants brought something new and vibrant to Ireland and helped the country to take virtually its first faltering steps towards the world outside. These steps were necessary. It was clear that Ireland's industrial problems could not be solved if there was total dependence on indigenous industries. The government decided that foreign entre-preneurs must be encouraged to come to Ireland. To that end and despite predictably strong opposition from the Department of Finance, it established the Industrial Development Authority (IDA) under the chairmanship of Dr Beddy in 1949. The new Authority initially had a rather varied shopping list, ranging from dealing with protective tariffs to creating and developing Irish industry but, in due course, it was given an expanded promotional role. It succeeded in persuading many industrialists, initially from mainland Europe, to set up operations in Ireland. The motivation of these continental industrialists may not have been entirely economic. They had just come through a terrible war and were among the lucky ones to have something left. They regarded Ireland, which had been neutral, as a suitable place of refuge in the event of another war driving them out of mainland Europe. At first, the IDA could offer them nothing of a monetary nature – only plenty of sound advice. It is a tribute to Beddy and his colleagues that, despite this limitation, they succeeded in bringing so many new industries to Ireland.

Any hope ICC might have had that some of these continental-owned companies would approach the market with public issues of shares was quickly dashed. Most of the companies were family-owned and had no experience of being listed on the stock exchanges in their own countries. It would be too much to expect that they would take what would be, to them, the gamble of letting the public in. When grants became available, there was even less incentive for these foreign-owned firms to go public. They would have perceived the grants as equity on which no dividend had to be paid.

While the establishment of the IDA was welcome and provided long-term benefits for the economy, there were immediate consequences for ICC. Dr Beddy, a key figure in ICC's development, now had to devote himself to building up the IDA and his regular attendance at ICC was no longer possible. ICC's accountant, M. M. Connor, was appointed acting company secretary (he was later to become company secretary). Although discharging his duties efficiently, Connor had a difficult task, especially as the company's chairman and managing director, J. P. Colbert, was in failing health and was to take early retirement soon afterwards. Fortunately, Colbert's health improved in later years and he had a happy and lengthy retirement until his death in 1975.

7

The Best was Yet to Come

Despite the establishment of the Industrial Development Authority (IDA), the economic gloom which had begun to gather towards the end of the 1940s continued throughout most of the 1950s. The inter-party government collapsed in 1951 and the Fianna Fáil government which replaced it embarked on a deflationary policy designed to repair the damage perceived to have been caused by balance of payments deficits. These deficits persisted throughout the 1950s largely because of the country's failure to generate an adequate level of exports.

An imaginative move by the new government was the establishment of An Foras Tionscal, a grant-giving agency for industrial development. Initially it was empowered to provide grants only in the under-developed areas west of the Shannon but, in 1959, its powers and geographical range were substantially extended, following a brief period during which the IDA handled new industry grants east of the Shannon. As in the case of the IDA, the chairman of An Foras Tionscal was Dr Beddy, who had returned to ICC as chairman and managing director following the retirement of Colbert in 1951. Beddy was thus simultaneously in charge of three important state-sponsored bodies – ICC, IDA and An Foras Tionscal. He was also chairman of the Commission on Emigration, which sat from 1948 to 1954. He coped with these hugely demanding tasks by working long hours during the week and by spending a large part of each weekend in his office, fortified only by frequent cups of tea and slices of his favourite fruitcake.

The establishment of An Foras Tionscal gave the IDA's work a new impetus as it could now accompany its honeyed words with the possibility of some free money. It was almost an article of faith with Beddy that grant-giving should be separate from promotional work, because he felt that a promotional body armed with a cheque-book would have great difficulty in refusing to grant-aid a project which it had been instrumental in attracting to the country. The contrary view, which prevailed after Beddy had retired from the IDA, was that it was easier for the industrialist to negotiate with one body rather than two and that, at any rate, it was unfair to people who had been encouraged to come to Ireland to expect them to persist with their project if their grant application was declined. One feels that if Gilbert and Sullivan had still been alive they might have enjoyed working with the concept of Beddy in his various incarnations as a kind of Pooh-Bah, Beddy of the IDA encouraging industrialists to come to Ireland, and Beddy of An Foras Tionscal refusing to give them grants!

This was a period of great difficulty for ICC. The new issue market, although not dried up, was nothing like as buoyant as it had been before and immediately after the war. Fewer companies were willing to go public and, besides, the period was one of economic gloom. Despite the unhappy state of the economy, ICC sponsored thirteen issues, which raised a total of £3.4 million during the 1950s. Until then, most of the flotations had been public issues or offers for sale but, with some of the companies originally floated reaching maturity, rights issues became more popular and four of the thirteen issues fell into that category.

ICC underwrote only one issue in 1950. However, it was to prove the most important issue in ICC's history, although it was not recognised as such at the time. Because of its importance, some background information may be of interest.

When Tom Roche's father died, Tom and his brother Donal set up a fruit and vegetable business to supplement the income their mother was deriving from operating as a newsagent in Inchicore in Dublin. It was not long before the entrepreneur in Tom Roche came to the fore. He began to deliver sand and gravel to builders and, even during the war years when petrol was hard to obtain, he managed to keep his customers satisfied. In the mid-1940s Tom and Donal set up the Castle Sand Company and this was immediately successful. However, major expansion was not possible because of limited capital resources. Having consulted the proprietors of Gypsum Industries to find out how they had dealt with their capital requirements, the Roches betook themselves to the offices of John Plunkett Dillon, Solicitor. With the aid of Dillon, and Robert Kidney of R. J. Kidney & Company, Auditors & Accountants, the brothers established Roadstone Limited. Its first act was to acquire from John A. Wood, of Cork, the quarry which he owned at the Hill of Allen. Satisfactorily for the Roches, John A. Wood took shares in Roadstone and became one of its directors, so no cash had to change hands. Thus began a friendship which was to blossom over the years.

In 1950 the Roche brothers called to see Dr Beddy, having been advised by Dillon that the ICC issue for Gypsum Industries a few years earlier had been very successful. This happened not long after I had joined ICC and I remember acting as the note-taker at some of these early meetings. To me the Roches were captains of industry, before whom I was awe-struck. How I appeared to them I do not know but they treated me with the kindness and consideration which, as I was to learn over the years, was an essential part of the Roche character. The issue was for what in the light of Roadstone's subsequent development was a modest figure, £241,000 – £50,000 in preference shares and £191,000 in ordinary shares. In today's terms this would be equivalent to a fund-raising of about £5 million. I remember that on the day the list of subscriptions opened I was sent to the National Bank, the receiving bank, to advise my superiors on how the issue had been received. I was full of enthusiasm and confidently expected heavy over-subscription. When I saw the figures, I was filled with a deep depression. Only 273 application forms had been received. The issue had been very much under-subscribed and ICC had what was then a huge underwriting liability of 21,050 preference shares and 91,450 ordinary shares. The company's solicitor, Dillon, was there when the bad news emerged and his reassuring (and prophetic) words 'you'll make money on those shares' are still ringing in my ears. ICC did make money and so did those few subscribers who had the courage to hold on to their shares.

Despite the comparative failure of the issue, Roadstone had raised the funds it needed and from then on it never looked back. It grew both organically and by acquisition, the latter including the Irish public company Clondalkin Concrete Limited, and the Liverpool company Forticrete Limited. During this period of significant growth, ICC provided considerable financial support and underwrote four further issues of shares for Roadstone. When Tom Roche launched his daring bid for Cement Limited in 1970, ICC through its subsidiary, Mergers Limited, provided advice to Roadstone. This was a great test of ICC's loyalty to Roadstone, because ICC had also enjoyed very friendly relations with Cement Limited, having brought it to the market in 1936 and underwritten three subsequent issues of Cement shares. However, since ICC could not advise both sides, a decision had to be made and support was offered to Roadstone. It will never be known whether, if the playing field had been left undisturbed, Roadstone would have succeeded in its giant-killer effort. However, a UK company, Readymix Limited, helped to hasten the conclusion of merger negotiations between Roadstone and Cement by making a bid for Roadstone. This had the effect of driving the two Irish-based companies into each other's arms and thus Cement-Roadstone Holdings Limited was born. CRH plc is now one of the leading shares in the Irish stock market and a major multi-national company.

The mutual respect which existed between Roche and Beddy was somewhat surprising. These two exceptional people were very different in their approach to business, although they were both shy and reluctant to seek publicity. Beddy was essentially an organisation man who believed in putting everything on paper and preferred a carefully thought-out project to one which was largely inspirational. Roche disliked formal procedures, intellectualised approaches to management and the production of masses of paper containing technical and accountancy jargon.

The Roadstone story has been told at some length for a number of reasons. Firstly, it illustrates the manner in which ICC, having decided to back an enterprise, stayed with it loyally through its various triumphs and occasional difficulties. Secondly, it is probably the outstanding mid-century story of the success of an Irish-owned firm which had limited financial resources but was driven by the vision and ambition of its founders. Thirdly, an account of Roadstone's success is probably the most eloquent tribute than can be paid to Tom Roche, who died in 1999. He did not believe in eloquent tributes and would have been embarrassed to read this. However, he deserves special appreciation because he was one of the first Irish industrialists to demonstrate that much can be achieved if one has the requisite ability and tenacity. He was also quick to recognise the talents of those who were to succeed him. When he retired from CRH, his entrepreneurial flair did not desert him. He carried out his own research and developed two new Liffey toll bridges, which have played an important role in easing Dublin's traffic problems.

Other outstanding native entrepreneurs have emerged in subsequent years – for example, Michael Smurfit, Tony O'Reilly, Tony Ryan, Neil McCann, Martin Naughton, Lochlann Quinn, and Denis O'Brien. But there were also some whose achievements are more directly comparable with the success of the Roche brothers. Three such fraternal examples are Brian and Conor Doyle of Fleetwood Limited, Gene and Brendan Murtagh of Kingspan plc, and Dan and Randall Tierney of the Cross Group.

There were other new ICC-sponsored issues in the 1950s which are worthy of note. In 1952 ACEC Ireland Limited, a Belgian-sponsored company which manufactured electric transformers and motors, raised £157,500 by way of an issue of preference shares. This provided a good example of how a foreign company could retain effective control despite the provisions of the Control of Manufactures Acts. The Irish company, which was located in Waterford, was set up with only a small amount of ordinary share capital, a majority of which was held by the company's solicitor. The bulk of the capital was in non-voting preference shares.

Another major issue in 1952 was for Irish Glass Bottle Company Limited. That company had been set up by the McGrath family in the 1920s but became a public company before the 1952 issue, which included a substantial equity element. It is worth noting that at the time of the Irish Glass Bottle issue, its subsidiaries included Waterford Glass Limited which, although relatively small, was already a cause for national pride because it was reviving an important craft industry of the nineteenth century. Some years later Waterford Glass was hived off as a separate entity, and Irish Glass Bottle Company is now part of the Ardagh Group. In the 1950s the brightly burning furnaces at Irish Glass Bottle Company's premises in Ringsend, Dublin, were a refreshing contrast to the business gloom which then seemed to be otherwise omnipresent.

Two other issues of the 1950s deserve mention. Aberdare Electric Company Limited (now Unidare) raised £275,000 in equity, and Tonge McGloughlin (Holdings) Limited raised £107,500 in preference shares. The Tonge McGloughlin issue is worthy of comment because it was probably the first holding company to raise capital in the Irish market. Other companies were holding companies in the sense that they had subsidiaries, but Tonge McGloughlin was an example of a company comprising two disparate subsidiaries which had come together for the purpose of raising capital that neither of them would have been large enough to raise separately. Tonge & Taggart operated an iron foundry business, while J. & C. McGloughlin had an unusual product mix – structural steel and church requisites.

With the exception of ACEC, all the companies mentioned were either wholly or predominantly Irish owned and controlled. This was a welcome development. Some of the companies launched in the 1930s were indigenous, but many were branches of British companies set up as separate entities in order to cope with Ireland's legislative requirements.

ICC's activities in the 1950s showed a much heavier emphasis on lending than in the preceding decades. However, ICC was suffering from a shortage of funds and its management betook themselves to the Department of Finance to seek an injection of much-needed capital. There they encountered the redoubtable J. J. McElligott who had many virtues and was, indeed, one of the giants involved in the development of the new state. However, he was very reluctant to spend any of the state's money and he took a fairly firm line with his visitors. He told ICC, in effect, to go and sell all that it had and only to come back when it had completely run out of money. This meant that there was a forced sale of shares which had been acquired largely as a result of underwriting activities. Because of the pressure to realise money, the shares were very often sold below market prices to institutions. It must have been galling for Beddy and others, who had helped to build up ICC's share portfolio, to see it being dissipated in this way and replaced very often by loans on which modest margins were earned or by new investments which took some time to reach the dividend-paying stage. Once ICC had complied with McElligott's suggestions, the department's attitude softened. It allowed an issue of ICC shares to raise £1 million (in three tranches between 1952 and 1957); as with earlier issues, most of these shares had to be taken up by the Minister for Finance.

Dr T. K. Whitaker, who worked closely with McElligott, and was, like him, to become secretary of the Department of Finance, wrote an appreciation of him after his death. McElligott's approach to ICC's problems is better understood when one reads in that appreciation that his 'long tenure of office as secretary of the Department of Finance was marked by tenacious adherence to the classical principle of curbing public expenditure and taxation' (Whitaker, 1983: p. 288). ICC was not the only organisation that crossed paths with McElligott and it is said that he was equally uncompromising with his own staff.

In 1955 the Fianna Fáil government fell and another inter-party government took over. The economy was still in the doldrums and the new government brought in export tax relief, whereby a company paid reduced tax on that portion of its profits which was derived from incremental exports. This was another step towards encouraging Irish industry to look outside the island for new markets. Unfortunately the economy remained in poor shape, with consequent emigration and the size of the home market reflecting the smaller population. The export tax relief was to provide a major stimulus to industry in later years, although its immediate impact was smaller than those who introduced it would have wished.

In 1957 the government changed again, with Fianna Fáil returning to power. In the previous year T. K. Whitaker had been appointed secretary of the Department of Finance and, under his guidance, the department in 1958 produced *Economic Development.* This document set forth a number of proposals designed to make the economy move forward. This publication led to the government's first programme for economic expansion, a programme which recognised that protectionism could be relied on no longer, especially if a free trade area was set up in Europe. Protection would, in future, be given only to those new industries which showed that they would soon be able to survive without protection. In 1958 the Industrial Development (Encouragement of External Investment) Act was passed, effectively wiping out the restrictions on foreign ownership of industry contained in the Control of Manufactures Acts of 1932 and 1934.

There was an important political event in 1959 when Éamonn de Valera, who had been either head of government or leader of the opposition since 1927, retired as Taoiseach and was elected President of Ireland. Seán Lemass, the dynamic Minister for Industry and Commerce, took his place. Given the outlook of Lemass, his appointment as Taoiseach was a virtual guarantee that the first programme for economic expansion would be vigorously implemented. As part of the programme, ICC was provided with more share and loan capital (a welcome change from the somewhat Dickensian approach adopted by McElligott) and was encouraged to increase its lending activities. The Minister for Finance, Dr Jim Ryan, announced that he would expect no dividend from ICC for ten years. As this might not be welcomed by individual shareholders, he offered to buy them out at par, an offer which was accepted by all but thirty-five shareholders. For the first time in its twenty-five years of existence, ICC was, at last, relatively flush with money. In chapter 8 we shall consider how ICC performed in the changed conditions of the 1960s.

It was of some importance to ICC that it changed its address from 9 Leinster Street to 26 Merrion Square in 1957. For twenty-four years, the company had occupied its less than palatial offices at Leinster Street. During the 1930s Colbert had attempted to move to a more suitable set of offices in St Andrew's Street, but had met with strong opposition when he tried to sell this idea to his fellow-directors who felt, predictably enough, that such a move would be unnecessarily extravagant.

The move to Merrion Square was not accomplished without much diplomacy on the part of Dr Beddy. A few years previously he had reached the conclusion that ICC needed new offices because the staff, though small, was increasing in number. He was aware that Arthur Cox, the well-known Dublin solicitor, owned 26 Merrion Square but was unwilling to sell it as it had been his mother's house up to the time of her death in 1953. The house was one of the first built in Merrion Square during the late 1770s. It had spacious, well-proportioned rooms, a number of ceilings with impressive plaster-work and, in general, an air of great distinction. Beddy eventually persuaded Cox to sell the premises to ICC, but Cox, who was a frequent visitor to ICC as solicitor to many of its customers, stipulated that, once the deal was completed, he should never again be expected to cross the threshold. As it happened, soon after the sale, Cox, who was notoriously absent-minded, made an appointment with ICC for one of his important clients and found himself in the building against his better judgement. Being both a pragmatist and a sentimentalist, he allowed some tears to fall, but felt free thereafter to ignore his self-imposed pre-condition to the sale.

ICC was very pleased to move to 26 Merrion Square. Beddy's discriminating appreciation of antique furniture ensured that its new offices were suitably and impeccably furnished, though at a modest cost. ICC remained in Merrion Square for nineteen years, until the mid-1970s when the growth in personnel forced it to seek more commodious premises once again.

During the 1950s ICC took the first serious steps towards augmenting its then very small staff, in terms of both numbers and expertise. Among the new recruits was Louis Heelan, who was at the time secretary of the Industrial Development Authority (IDA). He was appointed as a loan officer in 1953. Later in the decade Jack Ryan, then private secretary to T. K. Whitaker, joined the staff to head up the company's newly-established Machinery Finance Division. Both Heelan and Ryan made rapid progress in the company and, in due course, both became general managers, Ryan having previously been appointed company secretary in 1964 when Michael Connor retired. After Heelan retired in 1984 to pursue other interests, Ryan became deputy chief executive, a position he held until his retirement in 1990. Both Heelan and Ryan played a major part in the company's considerable progress during their periods of office.

Before we leave the 1950s, it is worth reflecting that this was a period during which ICC became involved in some of the new IDA-supported industries. An outstanding new enterprise of that era was the factory established in Killarney, County Kerry, by the German company Liebherr. This was welcome, not only for its own sake but also because the Liebherr Group was to become heavily involved in the tourist industry in Killarney, building two major hotels which are still among the finest in the country. Another successful company of the 1950s was Tabetex Limited, curtain fabric manufacturers, which was established in Shercock, County Cavan, by Italian entrepreneur Luciano Vergnano.

Naturally, not all the companies of that era have survived to the present day in their original form. For example, Chipboard Limited of Scarriff, County Clare, was set up in 1957 by the Aicher Brothers of Rosenheim in Bavaria; after twenty-seven years the Aichers went out of business, but the factory was taken over by a Spanish company and is now Finsa Limited. Another German-owned company, Jowika Limited of Listowel, County Kerry, manufacturers of sports knives and cutlery, which was set up in 1959, is today operated by a United States group under the name Imperial Schrade (Europe) Limited.

An important outcome of the establishment of these companies, whether they succeeded in their original form or not, is that they brought new expertise to the country and helped to develop skills in the various communities in which they operated.

The 1950s marked the conclusion of the first phase of ICC's development. The economy of the new state, which was fragile to begin with, suffered greatly from the effects of World War 2 and the recession of the 1950s. Despite this, ICC, from the time of its establishment in 1933, made a significant contribution to economic progress, particularly through its underwriting activities which enabled many companies, both new and more mature, to raise capital which would not otherwise have been readily available. As has been shown, the Irish stock market was relatively unimportant in Ireland's industrial life before 1933. ICC was a major contributor to the expansion of stock exchange activities and to the emergence and growth of a discerning investing public.

Probably the best way to illustrate the outlook of ICC in its early years is to quote an excerpt from a commemorative booklet issued by ICC during the 1960s:

> While ICC operates as a commercial undertaking and has been a profitable enterprise since its establishment, its primary aim is to contribute to national economic expansion. It examines sympathetically every project brought to its notice having regard particularly to economic soundness, employment potential, possible contribution to the reduction of emigration, importance to the proposed locality and utilisation of indigenous raw materials and of the services or products of existing industries. Its facilities have been availed of over the entire range of industry and in all parts of the country by large, medium and small undertakings. The small project receives as much attention as the large-scale development and ICC has grown up with many small concerns which are now leaders in their field. A high proportion of proposals are accepted and the company is continually seeking new ways of increasing its range of facilities and of encouraging and facilitating the development of Irish enterprise. It

maintains friendly and confidential relations with its clients and avoids involvement in day-to-day management. (Industrial Credit Company, 1969: pp 19-20)

8
The Buoyant Sixties –
A Tide Taken at the Flood

The 1960s were an exciting time. For Ireland, it was the most prosperous decade since Independence. The first programme for economic expansion was largely successful despite the failure of the agricultural sector to achieve the growth expected of it. Even though Ireland's first attempt to join the European Economic Community (EEC) failed, freer trade was in the air. Import tariffs were reduced in 1963 and 1964 and a new Anglo-Irish Trade Agreement, providing for reciprocal tariff abatements, was signed in 1965.

With freer trade approaching, the Minister for Industry and Commerce set up a Committee on Industrial Organisation which carried out detailed studies on the preparedness of various industries to live in an unprotected environment. These studies showed a need for re-equipment, and firms which were prepared to carry out such re-equipment were offered the choice of loans on special terms (through ICC) or adaptation grants (through An Foras Tionscal). While an attempt was made to make the financial effects of loans or grants roughly comparable, it was not surprising that the bulk of the applications were for grants rather than loans. By the end of the 1960s the economy was showing record growth rates, although the targets of the second programme for economic expansion, which had envisaged Ireland gaining EEC membership by 1970, were not being reached.

Socially and culturally the 1960s were infinitely more active than the previous decade. Telefís Éireann was launched at the end of 1961 and life was never the same thereafter for the people of Ireland. A forest of aerials attached to household chimneys indicated the desire of the populace to view television programmes originating in Great Britain but, with the establishment of a indigenous television service, it was no longer necessary to peer through snowy screens to watch a television programme. In 1963 such disparate celebrities as The Beatles and President John F. Kennedy of the United States came to Ireland. At home, showbands multiplied in number and displayed their talents in the many 'ballrooms of romance' which were established throughout the country. Culture was not neglected. The new Abbey Theatre and the Cork Opera House were opened in 1966 and 1967 respectively. The censorship of books was greatly eased and, by comparison with the past, a more liberal atmosphere prevailed in the country.

Under the auspices of Coras Tráchtála Teo, the Kilkenny Design Workshops were set up in 1963. This was the brainchild of Bill Walsh, then chief executive of Coras Tráchtála. Having had a study carried out by Scandinavian consultants, he set up the workshops in Kilkenny so that Irish and foreign designers could work together and thereby improve the quality of Irish industrial design. As a result, Irish industries derived great benefit and many of their products became saleable internationally for the first time. The Kilkenny Design Workshops closed in 1983, by which time a considerable improvement in Irish design had been achieved.

On the political front, Fianna Fáil were in government throughout the 1960s. Seán Lemass retired as Taoiseach in 1966 and was succeeded by Jack Lynch. Not everything went easily for the government. There were several major industrial disputes in the early part of the decade, and in 1966 the farmers made a well-publicised protest march to the Department of Agriculture.

An unfortunate social development, although it was not recognised as such at the time, was the opening of Ballymun flats in the late 1960s. Economic prosperity led to a building boom in which many well-known Dublin landmarks were dramatically altered. The Theatre Royal, the Regal Cinema and the original Electricity Supply Board offices in Lower Fitzwilliam Street were all casualties of the drive to rid the capital of old buildings and replace them with modern edifices.

ICC went into this new decade enjoying a good relationship with the Department of Finance. Throughout the period up to 1953, when McElligott was secretary of the department, and during the three subsequent years when O. J. Redmond was secretary, ICC's dealings with the department were very formal. The relationship between Whitaker and Beddy was a different matter. They admired each other greatly. In Appendix 2, with Dr Whitaker's consent, there is reproduced the text of a moving appreciation written by him on the occasion of Dr Beddy's death in 1976.

Even before the 1960s the support of Dr Whitaker had been obtained for the Irish banks to provide ICC with a long-term loan of £1.8 million on favourable terms. This represented a major step forward, as ICC had not previously enjoyed bank funding other than by way of temporary overdraft. The bank loan was guaranteed by the Minister for Finance but was still a major initiative in the context of the level of activity then undertaken by ICC. The Industrial Credit (Amendment) Act of 1958 had, for the first time, enabled the minister to subscribe directly for shares in ICC and to guarantee loans raised by the company. Previously the minister could acquire shares in ICC only by the cumbersome procedure of underwriting a public issue of the company's shares. Another Industrial Credit (Amendment) Act, passed in the following year, had increased ICC's authorised capital from £5 million to £10 million, increased its borrowing powers from £5 million to £15 million, and empowered the minister to make direct loans to ICC. In 1961 and 1962 the company's issued share capital was increased from £3 million to £8.8 million as a result of direct share subscription by the minister.

In response to representations from ICC and others, the Companies Act of 1959 included a provision whereby companies could issue redeemable preference shares. By that time, traditional preference shares, which had been the bread and butter of company financing during the 1930s and 1940s, had lost much of their appeal. Redeemable preference shares could be redeemed only out of profits or out of the proceeds of a fresh issue of shares. The provision enabled companies like ICC, which were unable to lend without security, to make an investment which bore a very strong resemblance to an unsecured loan. The power to take up redeemable preference shares was a welcome and valuable addition to the range of services which financial institutions like ICC could offer.

With its additional powers and resources, ICC was free to diversify in a way that had not been possible before and to face up to more serious competition. While it had been very active in the capital issues field, it really had only one competitor – Guinness Mahon & Company – and there was no major overlap between the activities of the two organisations. In lending, there had been no serious competition from the banks. ICC provided term loans, usually for ten years or more at fixed rates of interest. The banks favoured overdraft financing, which meant they were, in theory at any rate, short-term lenders (overdrafts tended in practice to echo the words of the song 'Kathleen Mavourneen' – 'It may be for years and it may be for ever').

The 1960s cover the early years of ICC's second phase of development and it is interesting to take a random survey of a few of the companies which developed in Ireland during that decade.

Leo Laboratories Limited of Dublin has been a successful branch operation of leading Danish owners since that time. Gernord Limited, Carrickmacross, County Monaghan, was set up in 1963 by a French company. It produces PVC vinyl flooring. A company which may have paved the way for the development of Irish cheese-making was Wexford Dairy Products Limited. It was established in 1964 by German owners and was the first Irish enterprise to produce Camembert-type cheese. Although it did not succeed in its original form, it has operated successfully for many years as Wexford Creamery under British ownership and management.

One of the many other companies which ICC helped to finance in the 1960s was Wavin Pipes Limited, which manufactures PVC piping. It deserves special mention because it represents a very effective blend of Irish entrepreneurship and foreign expertise. Wavin was partly owned by a group of Irish business people and partly by two Dutch institutions – Shell and a water authority. It is still an Irish/Dutch partnership, although Shell is no longer a shareholder, and the present managing director, Des Byrne, has paid gracious public tribute to the substantial support provided by ICC to the company, particularly during its formative years.

As part of its more aggressive marketing strategy, ICC decided in 1959 to enter the field of industrial hire-purchase. This was revolutionary for ICC in more ways than one. Firstly, it involved shorter-term lending (3–5 years) than had previously been customary. Secondly, ICC, which was accustomed to comprehensive security, was embarking on a type of financing where the only security was the machine purchased. Thirdly (and most important of all), ICC was entering into direct competition with established hire-purchase companies.

One of ICC's concerns has always been to give all relevant information to customers and potential customers. For that reason, it was decided that people buying equipment on hire-purchase should know what true rate of interest they were being asked to pay. Today the law requires companies offering credit facilities to show in their advertisements the true annual percentage rate (APR) charged. At that time, however, there was no such legal requirement and a favourite practice of those marketing hire-purchase was to attract customers with a prominently-displayed low interest rate. Many applicants were not sophisticated enough to perceive that the low rate was a 'flat' rate; in other words it was calculated on the entire principal for the three or four years of the agreement, even though monthly payments by the customers had the effect of continually reducing the capital outstanding. The effect of this was that a quoted rate of, say, 5 per cent would often work out as a true rate of the order of 10 per cent.

For ICC, however, there was to be no such quasi-deception. It determined that it would quote a true rate in its advertising and promotional literature. So it announced an attractive true rate of 6.5 per cent when others were quoting a flat rate of 5 per cent. One might have expected this full disclosure to lead to a queue of eager customers. On the contrary, however, few nibbled at the bait and some of those who did expressed with vehemence their detestation of the usurious rates which they thought ICC was charging compared with the rates being quoted elsewhere. Jack Ryan remembers being castigated by one customer whose triumphant parting shot was: 'You'll get no 6½ per cent from me'. ICC had to accept that, in a competitive world, appearance is everything and it too was soon advertising flat rates – to the obvious satisfaction of its customers. The hire-purchase business expanded rapidly and, by 1967, ICC had expanded its machinery finance activities to include equipment leasing. Asset financing has grown over the years and is an important and profitable part of ICC's business.

This new departure for ICC brought it into hitherto unknown spheres. Customers who, because of their size, would not have contemplated the formality of a term loan, were attracted by the idea of financing a machine by way of a simple procedure. Hire-purchase and leasing gave ICC access to a wider range of customers than it had previously enjoyed and increased the scope for selling its other services. One of the features of this form of financing is that it operates on fixed interest rates for the customers, but the hire-purchase provider usually borrows funds at variable rates. In a time of constantly changing rates, particularly when the movements are mostly in an upward direction, this can have serious financial implications for the provider of facilities unless it is carefully managed. It was at this time that ICC's Treasury division developed a new importance. This foreshadowed the significant role which that division has played in ICC's subsequent development.

In the years after the introduction of machinery finance, ICC ventured into more new territory by setting up two specialist subsidiary companies for the financing of film production and ship construction. The origins and history of these subsidiaries are described in chapter 9. Their establishment was an indication of ICC's willingness to enter into new and unfamiliar financial areas. However, they were, in a sense, side shows and should not deflect attention from the steps ICC took in the 1960s to develop its core businesses of underwriting and lending.

The pre-war fluency of new issues was never to return but, nevertheless, there had been nine new issues sponsored by ICC in the five years following the war. Even the stodgy 1950s had generated thirteen issues, many of them rights issues for existing public companies. The amount raised by these issues was approximately £3.5 million, including what was then a major fund-raising of £1.6 million by Cement Limited. In the more prosperous 1960s there were twenty flotations, which raised more than £11 million. Most of these were again rights issues, only a few companies becoming public for the first time during this buoyant period. Not surprisingly, four of the flotations (30 per cent of the total raised) were for the enterprising and capital-hungry Roadstone Limited. A company which came to the market for the first time in the 1960s was Glen Abbey Limited, which for many years operated successfully under the direction of its two founders, the brothers Colm and Rory Barnes. Other familiar names which made ICC-sponsored issues during the 1960s were Cement Limited, Arklow Pottery Limited, Sunbeam Wolsey Limited and Clondalkin Paper Mills Limited.

On the lending side, ICC, with improved funding, was able to become much more active than in the past. At the beginning of the 1960s (twenty-seven years after the establishment of ICC), ICC's total loans to industry amounted to £4.3 million. At the end of the decade, that figure had increased almost four-fold to £15.3 million. The build-up of activities in the 1960s was, of course, facilitated by the growth generated in the economy by the implementation of the government programmes for economic expansion. At the 1966 annual general meeting of ICC, the chairman pointed out that, whereas in 1958 the balance sheet of ICC consisted of loans (20 per cent) and shares (80 per cent), those percentages had been virtually reversed in less than a decade.

The substantial expansion by ICC occurred even though it was encountering serious competition for the first time. The increasingly healthy state of the Irish economy encouraged banks from outside the country to take an interest. In 1965 First National City Bank (now Citibank) opened a branch in Dublin and in the following year the Bank of Nova Scotia arrived. In the meantime, the Northern Bank had been acquired by the Midland Bank. Two major domestic mergers were also completed: the Bank of Ireland, which had acquired the Hibernian Bank in 1958, acquired the Irish section of the National Bank in December 1965; and in 1966 Allied Irish Banks came into existence as a result of the merger of the Munster & Leinster Bank, the Provincial Bank and the Royal Bank. Later, other foreign banks, notably the First National Bank of Chicago (which subsequently withdrew), the Bank of America, Banque Nationale de Paris and ABN AMRO, also came to Ireland.

It would be an exaggeration to say that the newly-arrived banks were given a traditional Irish welcome. On the contrary, the banking system as a whole was concerned about this foreign competition and ICC, like the other indigenous financial institutions, did not take any steps to form part of a welcoming committee. Nevertheless, it has to be admitted that these newcomers probably had a disproportionate influence for good on the Irish financial scene. Firstly, they brought with them what would then have been regarded as an aggressive mentality which caused them to seek business rather than wait for it to come to them. Secondly, they introduced into banking the concept of the term loan, something which ICC had offered since its establishment but which now, marketed by others, constituted a competitive threat. Thirdly, their appraisal techniques were somewhat more streamlined than those previously in use in Ireland.

ICC took the new-found competition in its stride after overcoming its initial reaction to these 'blow-in' bankers. Although never a monopoly in the conventional sense, ICC had up until then operated in a benign competitive climate.

Now the competition was real and earnest. It was good for ICC as, indeed, it was for the Irish banks and business in general. Since the 1960s ICC has lived in an increasingly competitive environment. Its ability to cope with that competition has been clearly demonstrated by the manner in which its trading results have improved over the years.

At the beginning of the 1960s the government had set up the National Industrial and Economic Council. It had a series of studies carried out, including one on the distributive sector. That study found that the greatest financial Cinderella in the economy was the sector comprising wholesalers and retailers. It urged that arrangements be made to provide adequate capital for this important group. ICC accepted the challenge and, for the first time in its history, commenced lending to firms engaged in trade rather than industry. The Memorandum and Articles of ICC empowered it to lend to any trade or industry. This had been interpreted up until then to mean only manufacturing industry, although the production of films was deemed to fall into that category. All over the country, there are large and small wholesalers and retailers who have reason to be grateful to ICC for this formalised extension of its activities through the introduction of a 'Finance for Distribution' scheme in 1968.

While ICC has customers throughout the distributive sector, it is worth noting that one of its first contacts in this sector was with the Musgrave Group. Under the dynamic direction of its chairman Hugh Mackeown, that group has expanded considerably over the years. Through its Super Valu and Centra outlets, the group is supplier to a significant part of the Irish grocery trade. It also operates major cash-and-carry wholesale centres for the independent retailer.

The final years of the 1960s saw some other developments which were important for ICC. One of these was the opening in Cork of ICC's first branch office. As ICC had never set out to be a retail bank, the provision of a branch network was far from its thoughts during its first thirty-five years. ICC was always willing to visit potential customers in whatever part of the country they lived and, indeed, a visit to the applicant's premises was deemed essential before any financial commitment was undertaken. However, those who lived outside the Dublin area often had to make the journey to Dublin when they were negotiating financial facilities. With the growth in business, it became clear that a presence in Munster would be desirable and, in 1969, a branch office was opened on the South Mall in Cork. The office was small and quite unimpressive, but the mere fact that ICC was present in Cork stimulated a good deal of new business in the Munster area. One of the less desirable features of the office was that it was immediately adjacent to a bus stop and when it rained (which seemed to occur almost every day in 1969), citizens of Cork used the entrance to ICC's new offices as a bus shelter. Modest though the office was, its existence emphasised ICC's increasing commitment to regional development.

The Cork office was subsequently moved twice. A few years later, a floor became available in a building occupied by Citibank on the opposite side of the South Mall, but ICC agonised over whether it was wise for two institutions in competition with each other to share the same building. Eventually these doubts were resolved and the Cork branch of ICC made its first move. Some time later the opportunity to acquire a fine premises at the corner of South Mall and Grand Parade presented itself. ICC occupies this building to the present day. One small problem was that the Legion of Mary had been the previous occupants and there was a large statue of the Blessed Virgin Mary on the front wall over the entrance. For a business which dealt more with Mammon than with God, the continued presence of the statue – excellent statue though it was – was scarcely appropriate. It was feared that if the statue were removed in broad daylight, there might well be an adverse reaction, especially since it was not unusual for groups of people to hold prayer meetings on the street in front of the building. A solution was found when one of ICC's directors arranged for his staff to remove the statue during the night. It was donated to a local convent where, so far as I am aware, it still reposes.

Another event of the 1960s was the setting up of Táiscí Stáit Teoranta (TST) by the government. Its purpose was to undertake large-scale investments in projects which, though desirable from a national standpoint, involved a high degree of commercial risk. The literal translation of the new company's name was 'State Treasures Limited', but this was a bit of a misnomer since most of the investments held by TST were either too large or carried too high a risk for ICC, with its limited capital resources, to undertake. Accordingly, investments in both the Industrial Engineering Company Limited and Verolme Cork Dockyard, which had been held by ICC on behalf of the state, were transferred to TST and formed part of its initial portfolio. The board of TST was a high-powered team, consisting of the secretaries of the departments of Finance, Industry and Commerce, Agriculture, and Transport and Power. ICC was not represented on the board of TST, but provided administrative and clerical services to it. When Fóir Teoranta was established in 1972, the assets (such as they were) of TST were transferred to the new company.

In 1969 ICC set up a subsidiary Mergers Limited (now ICC Corporate Finance Limited) to take over the issuing house services provided by ICC and to offer corporate financial advice, particularly in the areas of mergers and takeovers. This new subsidiary was set up primarily to ensure that customers of ICC, who needed specialist financial advice, would know that such advice was available from within the ICC group. ICC took what was at the time an unusual step for an Irish state-sponsored body by inviting a British resident – Sir Charles Ball, then chief corporate finance adviser in Kleinwort Benson – to join the board of Mergers Limited. Sir Charles, who was Irish by birth, made a valuable contribution to the new subsidiary, particularly in its advisory work. One of the most important transactions in which he was involved was the Roadstone bid for Cement Limited in 1970. The board of the new subsidiary also included Guy Jackson, assistant managing director of Guinness Ireland. He was a highly-esteemed member of the board and his untimely death (he was one of several prominent Irish businessmen killed in the dreadful Staines air crash of 1972) was a great blow to all who knew him. It was particularly poignant for his colleagues that, on the Friday before the air crash, he had written a letter setting

At an early AGM of ICC (members of the first Board in bold)

Standing L to R: *J. M. Fitzgerald (Auditor); Hubert Briscoe (Stockbroker); M. M. Connor (Accountant);* **John F. Punch;** *James P. Beddy (Secretary);* **Dr. Lawrence J. Kettle;** *John S. O'Connor (Solicitor); Esmonde O'Brien (Stockbroker).*
Seated L to R: **J. J. O'Leary;** *John Leyden (Secretary - Department of Industry & Commerce);* **John P. Colbert** *(Chairman & Managing Director);* **Tim Caffrey;** *J. J. McElligott (Secretary - Department of Finance).*

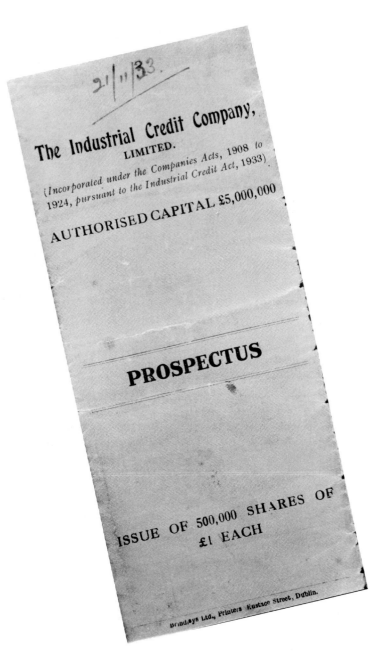

ICC's first Prospectus, November 1933

The Subscription List will open on **Tuesday, November 21st, 1933, and will close on or before Saturday, November 25th, 1933.**

The Minister for Finance has agreed under Section 5 of the Industrial Credit Act, 1933, to take up and pay for any Shares not subscribed for by the public on or before Saturday, November 25th, 1933.

Application will be made to the Committee of the Dublin Stock Exchange for permission to deal in the undermentioned Shares and in due course for an official quotation.

The Industrial Credit Company, Limited

(Incorporated under the Companies Acts, 1908 to 1924, pursuant to the Industrial Credit Act, 1933).

AUTHORISED CAPITAL, £5,000,000

(Divided into 5,000,000 Shares of £1 each.

(The present is the first Issue made by the Company.)

ISSUE OF 500,000 SHARES OF £1 EACH

The Bank of Ireland, College Green, Dublin, and Branches, as Bankers to the Company, are authorised to receive applications for the above-mentioned 500,000 shares, payable as follows :—

On Application	5/- per share
On December 15th, 1933	15/- „ „
	£1 per share

DIRECTORS.

JOHN PATRICK COLBERT, Mount Merrion House, Stillorgan Road, Blackrock, Co. Dublin (*Chairman and Managing Director of The Agricultural Credit Corporation, Ltd.*) (*Chairman and Managing Director*).

TIMOTHY CAFFREY, Willowfield, Cross Avenue, Blackrock, Co. Dublin (*Managing Director, National City Bank, Ltd. Managing Director, The Property Loan and Investment Company, Ltd.*).

LAURENCE JOSEPH KETTLE, 6 Mountainview Road, Ranelagh, Dublin, S.W.9 (*Consulting Engineer*).

JOHN JOSEPH O'LEARY, 43 Parkgate Street, Dublin (*Managing Director, Cahill and Co., Ltd.*).

JOHN FRANCIS PUNCH, 7/8 Academy Street, Cork (*Managing Director, Punch and Co., Ltd.*).

BANKERS.

BANK OF IRELAND, College Green, Dublin, C.I.

SOLICITORS.

JOHN S. O'CONNOR, 7 Upper Ormond Quay, Dublin, N.W.8.

BROKERS.

ESMONDE O'BRIEN, 1 College Street, Dublin, C.4.
BUTLER AND BRISCOE, 16,17 College Green, Dublin, C.I.

AUDITORS.

KEVANS AND SONS, 43 Upper O'Connell Street, Dublin, C.8.

SECRETARY AND REGISTERED OFFICES.

JAMES PATRICK BEDDY, 9 Leinster Street, Dublin, C.17.

ICC's first Prospectus, November 1933

Finishing department – polishing forks and spoons – at Newbridge Cutlery Limited, an ICC stock market flotation in 1935.

View of factory, Irish Wire Products Limited, Limerick which was introduced to the stock market by ICC in 1935.

Fine sisal spinning, Irish Ropes Limited, Newbridge, County Kildare (now part of the Barlo Group) – an ICC investment in the 1930s.

Part of moulding section, showing the conveyor system at Waterford Ironfounders Limited – floated as Allied Ironfounders (Ireland) Limited by ICC in 1936.

Part of Cement Limited works at Drogheda, County Louth. ICC introduced Cement Limited to the market in 1936.

Unloading beet at Cómhlucht Siúicre Éireann Teoranta (Irish Sugar Company) Carlow factory in the early 1940s. The company had progressed steadily since ICC floated it in the mid 1930s.

Sewing room at Prices Tailors (Ireland) Limited, Dublin a substantial employer in the early 1940s, having been introduced to the stock market by ICC in 1935.

Part of quarry and plant, Southern Chemicals Limited, Askeaton, County Limerick. The company became a customer of ICC during the 1940s, producing calcium carbide required for the transport and engineering industries which was in short supply during World War 2.

Doubling cotton yarns at Braids Limited, Ennis, County Clare – a significant employer in the mid-West by the 1940s, having been introduced to the market by ICC in 1938.

Clicking Room (cutting leather for uppers) at John Rawson & Sons (Ireland) Limited, Dundalk, County Louth which was floated by ICC on the stock market in 1947.

Plaster board machine at Gypsum Industries Limited, Kingscourt,
County Cavan, which ICC also brought to the market in 1947.

Section of spinning department, Cloth Manufacturers Limited,
Cootehill, County Cavan in the early 1950s,
a company supported by ICC.

Loading stone at quarry face, Roadstone Limited – floated by ICC in 1950.

Winding department, A.C.E.C. (Ireland) Limited, Waterford – a Belgian-sponsored company brought to the market by ICC in 1952.

Wire-drawing department at Aberdare Electric Company Limited (now Unidare), Finglas, Dublin. ICC sponsored a share issue for the company in 1953.

Sawing heavy girder at Upper Sheriff Street, Dublin works of J. & C. McGloughlin Limited, part of Tonge McGloughlin (Holdings) Limited floated by ICC in 1954, possibly the first holding company to do so on the Irish market.

A selection of ICC sponsored prospectuses.

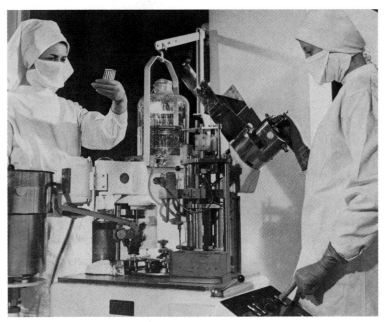

"Fastocain" Dental Cartridges being filled and sealed under sterile conditions at Leo Laboratories Limited, Dublin, which became a customer of ICC in the early 1960s.

ICC's Headquarters at 26 Merrion Square, Dublin from 1957 to 1976.

Shooting a scene from
The Playboy of the Western World
- a feature film financed by Irish
Film Finance Corporation Limited in
the early 1960s.

The launching of the New Adventure *– a ship financed by Shipping Finance Corporation Limited – at Verolme Cork dockyard in the mid 1960s.*

out his views on a matter with which Mergers was then concerned. The letter arrived on the Monday after the crash. After Guy Jackson's death, the managing director of Guinness Ireland, Dr Arthur Hughes, agreed to join the board of Mergers Limited and the company enjoyed the benefit of his wisdom and experience until his retirement in 1979.

The establishment of Mergers Limited came towards the end of a decade when ICC was still the major operator in the new issues market, a situation that would shortly change. There is a general belief that underwriting is an easy way for a financial institution to make profits, especially in boom times when there is a hunger for new shares, but there can be unexpected difficulties. One of ICC's experiences illustrates the point. A relatively small company with a good trading record asked ICC to underwrite a flotation and this was agreed in principle. For the purpose of this narrative, the company is given the name 'Incognito Limited', because it is still in existence and trading satisfactorily.

At the time when ICC agreed to participate, the accounts of 'Incognito' for the previous year were not available. However, management anticipated maintenance of the company's steady growth and, on their previous record, their expectation was thought to be well founded. There is a section in every prospectus which deals with a subject that is very important to the prospective investor, that is, the extent to which anticipated dividends will be covered by profits. Because of the absence of the latest accounts, ICC prepared a draft paragraph which said that, on the basis of the net profit for the latest year, and after making such adjustments as were appropriate, the cover for the proposed dividend of 'Incognito' would be *** times. When the accounts finally appeared in the week before scheduled publication, it was found that the profits were threadbare. When the blank was filled in, the cover for dividend was 0.2 times – a long distance from the three-fold cover that had been anticipated. It did not take long for all parties to agree that a flotation would be inadvisable and a less glamorous financing package had to be arranged. The 'Incognito' prospectus, although never published, enjoys a special place in the memories of all in ICC who were associated with it.

In a more serious vein, it can be recorded that in the thirty-five years from ICC's inception to 1968, it was responsible for underwriting 54 per cent of the capital raised by way of stock exchange flotations in the Irish market. The number of such ICC-sponsored flotations also exceeded 50 per cent of the total. Of the ten largest industrial companies, seven had availed of the underwriting and issuing house services provided by ICC.

In 1969, with the encouragement and support of the Minister for Finance, ICC introduced a special loan scheme for firms that had too small an equity base to warrant borrowing on commercial terms on the scale required. The scheme was entitled 'Finance for Undercapitalised Concerns', an unfortunate title in a period when an acronym was found for almost every organisation, institution or scheme. Whatever its title defects, the scheme was imaginative. The financial requirements of a beneficiary company were satisfied by two categories of loan – Loan A and Loan B. Loan A was provided on normal ICC terms, but Loan B involved deferment of principal repayments and sometimes even postponement of interest payments. The Loan B part of these transactions was dealt with by way of a special arrangement with the Department of Finance. It was a measure of the improved relationship and greater trust that then existed between ICC and its sponsoring department that the decision on what the size of Loan B should be was left to ICC. Needless to say, ICC did not abuse the department's trust.

The 1960s proved to be the most successful decade economically for the Republic since the establishment of the state. They were also years of spectacular growth for ICC. This growth was accompanied by a significant rise in the number of people ICC employed. Many of the new recruits were young and inexperienced university graduates, but there were also several executives who came from the world of business. Their contribution was invaluable since they had experience of the problems faced by industry and could, for instance, readily understand the panic which would be caused by the lack of sufficient monies to enable a customer to pay Friday's wages.

Another piece of new ground broken during the 1960s was the appointment of ICC's first woman executive – thirty-two years after the foundation of the company. Today ICC has many women in key positions, including the company secretary, Pauline McLaughlin; the law agent, Clare Connellan; the group economist, Mary Doyle; and the deputy group treasurer, Imelda Malynn.

In 1969 Dr J. P. Beddy, who had been chairman and chief executive since 1952, retired and I became general manager. Beddy remained as non-executive chairman until 1972 and so for the first three years of my new appointment, I had access to Beddy's advice. Chapter 12 deals further with Beddy, whose part in the development of ICC and other organisations was considerable.

9

A Tale of Two Subsidiaries

In the late 1950s ICC had provided long-term finance towards the establishment of Ardmore Studios. It soon became apparent to the founders and directors of Ardmore, Louis Elliman and Emmett Dalton, that there was no queue of film-makers wishing to use the studios. They believed that a major inhibiting factor was finance. Film-makers often had enough resources to finance, say, 15 per cent of a film and they could generally borrow 50–55 per cent from banks on the security of the film itself. What was lacking was 'end money', that is, the amount required to complete the financing of the film. In the United Kingdom, the National Film Finance Corporation existed for this purpose and it was claimed that, in addition to discharging its main function of encouraging film-makers to use British studios, it had many financial successes. The end money provider, although at the end of the queue for repayment of its advances, could fare very well if the film proved successful.

In 1960 ICC was persuaded to set up a subsidiary, Irish Film Finance Corporation Limited (IFFC), to provide end money for films made at Ardmore. Never was there a more apt description than 'end money'. The new subsidiary was to learn that the film-makers it encountered had a very simplistic approach to finance, involving considerable expenditure on their own part and a relaxed attitude towards the unfortunate providers of end money. If a film as popular as *Four Weddings and a Funeral* had been made at Ardmore, then IFFC would have prospered. Unfortunately there was no such success and losses accumulated. Out of fifteen films financed between 1960 and 1962, only a few small and unmemorable productions succeeded in paying their way. Even their titles indicate that they have been and are probably best forgotten – *Enter Inspector Duval*, *A Guy Called Caesar* and *Freedom to Die* are some random examples. It is unlikely that the average gross income of each of these films exceeded £100,000. This is some distance from the $1.8 billion achieved by director James Cameron's film of the late 1990s, *Titanic*.

The adverse financial position of IFFC was aggravated when its chairman, C. Russell Murphy, conceived the idea of IFFC itself financing and producing a film. The chosen film was *The Playboy of the Western World* and an impressive cast, including Siobhán McKenna as Pegeen Mike, was assembled. The film was not a major financial success, although for years afterwards ICC received small royalty payments in respect of showings of the film, mainly in universities throughout the United States.

The *Playboy* was IFFC's last serious attempt at film financing and caused Dr Beddy in his chairman's statement to the 1965 annual general meeting of ICC, to say:

> We knew at the time [of setting up IFFC] that the venture would be fraught with special risks. Our experience suggests that the net national advantage in providing this type of film is conjectural. Our initial adventure in this field has demonstrated that there are exceptional risks involved and this must influence our attitude towards further provision of film finance unless it is reasonably clear that the result will be of net national benefit.

Despite what Beddy said, IFFC was not a total failure. Without its activities, it is unlikely that Ardmore, which is still in existence though under different ownership, would have survived. It is also permissible to wonder whether the successes of several Irish-made films in recent years would have been as great if no pioneering work had been undertaken in the 1960s.

Recalling the activities of IFFC conjures up a picture of ICC trying to steer a course between the Scylla of Ardmore Studios and the Charybdis of IFFC. The chairman of

Ardmore was T. F. Laurie, a former chief executive of Esso Ireland Limited. He was a very able administrator, but was probably too accustomed to business formality to fit happily into the Bohemian world of film production. It is said that, when presiding at board meetings, he would, with old-world courtesy, enquire 'Is it your will and your pleasure that I sign these minutes?' He found the exotic film industry somewhat hard to take. On one occasion he disgustedly brought into ICC the script of a proposed film with a title like 'Black Stockings for Chelsea', and asked for sympathy for having to consider such unadulterated filth. From a financial point of view, it is probable that such a film would have been a box-office success and, therefore, a suitable subject (commercially) for IFFC financing. Instead of this, Russell Murphy and his colleagues had to consider decent though uninspiring offerings, most of which they were forced to reject.

As Russell Murphy has been the subject of much criticism since his death, it is only fair to say that, from ICC's point of view, he was a competent chairman, although somewhat eccentric. He used to say that he was at his happiest during a long holiday weekend, when he could spend all three days in the office without any danger of interruption. He was known primarily for his work as a receiver and liquidator and had a number of successful operations in this field. He was a tall, pale man and always dressed in black. At the beginning of one of his liquidations, a clerk in the distressed company, who had lost a previous job as a result of an earlier Russell Murphy liquidation, marked his arrival by likening him to 'f...ing Dracula'.

When it was clear that IFFC would not be financing any more films, Russell Murphy made the following statement to the 1968 annual general meeting of IFFC:

> The changing taste of the public has perhaps been the most serious adverse factor. Whereas in the past, the cinema has provided an escape from the drab realities and offered freedom and fantasy at a nominal cost, the affluent society of today is more inclined to remain in the comfort of the home or, alternatively,

to avail of the facilities of modern transport. In either event, the cinema does not come into the reckoning.

Warming to his theme, Russell Murphy referred to the

> ...additional hardship that people today want to be entertained and not to think. A film or a play must not make any demands on the mental powers of a customer. This eliminates the medium-budget film and restricts profit-making possibilities to costly epics with international appeal.

Soon after the effective demise of IFFC (it was not formally wound up until many years later), a committee was set up under the chairmanship of John Huston to consider the future of the Irish film industry. From the deliberations of that committee sprang the Irish Film Board. ICC's link with the film world was continued by the appointment of one of ICC's general managers, Louis Heelan, as the first chairman of that board. Heelan recalls that *Angel*, a feature film directed by one of Ireland's most successful directors, Neil Jordan, was one of the first films for which the new board provided finance.

Before leaving the world of film financing, it is pleasant to record that during the 1990s, after many years of abstention from the delights and risks of film financing, ICC invested successfully in two films – *Michael Collins* and *The Butcher Boy*. These investments were made on a strictly commercial basis – a far cry from the dismal 'end money' days of IFFC.

Soon after the establishment of IFFC, ICC set up another subsidiary – Shipping Finance Corporation Limited. In 1960 the Taoiseach Seán Lemass had invited Cornelis Verolme to take over and develop the dockyard at Rushbrooke near Cobh, County Cork. Verolme was a self-made and successful Netherlands shipbuilder, who had developed shipyards in his native country and abroad. By the 1960s he had become very arrogant and he made it clear that he would require considerable encouragement to undertake something that was not on his busy agenda. In his autobiography he tells how he came to Cobh and inspected the shipyard.

It was a very old yard which, in the days of the English, had been used as a naval shipyard with a dry dock. About 70 men were working there but, at about 10 o'clock in the morning, there were about 40 drunk at the gate already and the others were pottering around a little. My impressions could only be negative. (Verolme, 1975: p. 110)

Despite this initial adverse reaction, he saw potential in the yard and, encouraged by government subsidies, developed a shipyard capable of constructing cargo vessels of up to 70,000 tonnes. Although his impression of the workers was initially unflattering, he later came to realise that he had reached too hasty a judgement: 'I must say that the Irish labourers do remarkably good work, that the efficiency at this yard is at a high level, that the wage level is favourable and that we can compete on the international market . . . additionally, it is one of the most beautiful shipyards in the world' (Verolme, 1975: pp 112–113).

Although Verolme regarded his Irish shipyard as internationally competitive, it soon became apparent that, without finance for ship owners, it would not be possible for the yard to obtain business against the Japanese and Korean yards or even against the more expensive traditional shipbuilding countries like Germany and Britain, where there was no shortage of finance. ICC's new subsidiary, Shipping Finance Corporation (SFC), filled this gap by offering substantial funds (up to 80 per cent of cost) to ship-owners ordering vessels from Irish yards. The outcome was financially much more satisfactory than in the case of the Irish Film Finance Corporation. Ships (mostly of 30,000 tonnes or more) were financed for Irish, Canadian, South African, American, Danish, German and Liberian owners and this activity contributed significantly to Ireland's developing exports. In only one case was there any difficulty about repayment and, even then, the outcome was not adverse because the ship was sold on satisfactory terms.

Through SFC, ICC learned that ship financing had its own special features, in particular the need to contend with unscrupulous middlemen, whose interest in having a ship built was entirely related to the amount of commission which could be creamed off. The chairman of SFC, A. L. (Leo) Downes, was a successful businessman but was of a trusting disposition, and did not always appreciate that SFC was being asked to satisfy the demands of a greedy promoter. His finest hour occurred one day in a Dublin hotel when he met by appointment a negotiator whose only motive for introducing the business to SFC was to seek a huge commission for himself. This gentleman pretended that he loved Ireland dearly and was very anxious to have a ship built in this country. He was less than pleased when he was taken at face value by Downes, who failed to offer him the substantial commission for which he had been hoping.

Downes was a major hotelier in Cork – chief executive of the Imperial Hotel – and a member of Bord Fáilte. He was very knowledgeable about the hotel business and had a keen financial brain, which he brought to bear with considerable success on the activities of SFC. His loyalty to his native Cork was never in doubt. On one occasion the board of SFC visited the huge Verolme dockyard in Rotterdam. One of Downes' Dublin colleagues opined that the Dutch dockyard was so large that it could accommodate several Cork dockyards. 'It could take far more Dublin dockyards', Downes replied dryly, but with a characteristic twinkle in his eye.

In 1976 SFC financed its largest vessel, a 70,000-tonne bulk-carrier for Danish owners. As with all ship launchings, the launch in Rushbrooke was a spectacular occasion. Irish people who were present were proud to see that this huge vessel had been produced by Irish workers. It was sad that the dockyard would soon cease shipbuilding as Verolme found it impossible to withstand international competition. With the ending of shipbuilding at Rushbrooke, the need for SFC naturally disappeared.

10
The Seventies –
Oil and Troubled Waters

The first three years of the 1970s were reasonably good for the economy, although they started unpropitiously, as the following extract from the chairman's statement to the 1971 annual general meeting of ICC shows:

> ... a period during which the national economy was affected adversely and the rate of growth in GNP declined because of circumstances of a character, degree and magnitude not previously experienced, e.g., rapidly mounting inflation, higher long-term interest rates, a 21-week cement strike and a 27-week bank closure.

In 1972 a budget deficit was planned and incurred by the state. This deviation from orthodoxy was as nothing compared to the series of much heavier budget deficits recorded in the remainder of the 1970s. A new Fine Gael/Labour government came into office in 1973, immediately after Ireland had joined what was then the European Economic Community (EEC). The new government was soon beset by the oil crisis, which pushed oil prices up four-fold and had an adverse effect on the finances of most Western countries. Nationally, the agricultural sector benefited from the Common Agricultural Policy and this offset, to some extent, the unpleasant effects of what was happening in the oil world. In 1972, before the oil crisis, inflation was already high at 11 per cent, but in the two subsequent years, it rose to 17 per cent and then to 21 per cent. The government felt it had little option but to accept as the norm large budget deficits and enormous foreign borrowings.

This abandonment of traditional financial orthodoxy did not end with the landslide election of a new Fianna Fáil government in 1977. Budget deficits continued to be the order of the day and the trend was aggravated by the second oil crisis in 1979, the year in which Jack Lynch resigned and was replaced as Taoiseach by Charles J. Haughey.

Throughout the period the reconstituted Industrial Development Authority was extremely active. The Industrial Development Act of 1969 had given it very wide powers and it vigorously set about the task of attracting more multinational companies to Ireland. A far-sighted decision was taken to give special emphasis to the electronic and pharmaceutical sectors. While the beneficial effects of this decision were not immediately apparent, the economy as a whole has, in more recent years, greatly gained from the priority given to these two growth sectors.

ICC was naturally affected by the national and international events of the 1970s. The bank strikes and the oil crises of the 1970s were unwelcome to ICC and its customers, particularly small and medium-sized industries. The six-month bank strike of 1970 inevitably led to an increase in bad debts, but not to an extent that was calamitous for ICC and most of its customers. The huge increase in oil prices in 1973 imposed a bigger strain on business and naturally led to enormous working capital requirements at a time when wholesale interest rates were rising steadily, peaking at over 16 per cent. ICC pursued a prudent but helpful policy in meeting these exceptional customer demands and, notwithstanding all the difficulties, can look back with satisfaction on the decade as a period during which the company was able to build upon the achievements of the 1960s.

In 1970 ICC provided £4.85 million for industry. This was the second highest amount provided up to then in the company's history, the highest figure having been £5.6 million in the previous year. The main problem for ICC was finding a way of raising enough funds to enable it to contribute more fully to national prosperity. The Minister for Finance had been given power to make repayable advances to ICC, but up to now there was no opportunity to ask the public to involve themselves in the financing of ICC other than through public issues of its own shares which, as we have seen, did not result in a rush of applications.

In 1968 the first tentative steps had been taken towards the acceptance of deposits from the public. Because of the lack of a branch office network, it was decided not to seek small deposits. A minimum of £1,000 per deposit (the equivalent of almost £10,000 in today's terms) was fixed, but amounts substantially in excess of this were sought and obtained, mainly from the corporate sector. The attractiveness of the deposit scheme was enhanced by a state guarantee, although this guarantee has never been invoked. While the move into deposits may have seemed, at the time, a relatively minor development, it had great long-term significance as, over the years, deposits became a very important source of funds for ICC.

In 1971, after much detailed negotiation, a loan of US$10 million was arranged with the World Bank. Although it seems a small amount today, this loan was most welcome and enabled ICC to provide long-term credit on favourable terms to many under-capitalised industries. In the same year, contact was made with the European Investment Bank (EIB) as a prelude to the applications which ICC would make to that institution when the country became a member of the EEC.

The year 1972 saw the winding up of Táiscí Stáit Teoranta and the establishment of Fóir Teoranta. As is shown in chapter 11, Fóir did much good work during its existence but it was inevitable, given the nature of its customer base, that there was a high failure rate and it was eventually wound up in 1990. ICC took over the management of the remaining investments and borrowings of Fóir Teoranta on behalf of the government.

In 1973 Ireland became a fully-fledged member of the EEC, and ICC marked this by negotiating a £2.5 million loan from the EIB. This was the first of many loans which were to be arranged over the years with EIB. If the loan of £2.5 million was the first loan from EIB, a loan of US$30 million negotiated with the World Bank in the following year was to be the last from that source, since Ireland was now regarded by the World Bank as having reached a stage of development where further support was unnecessary. Besides, the World Bank felt, not unreasonably, that as Ireland was now a member of the EEC, it was up to that community to look after the needs of investment banks in its constituent countries (like ICC in Ireland) through its own investment bank. The final World Bank loan was ear-marked for the benefit of small and medium-sized enterprises and provided ICC with essential funds for carrying out its core business. It is a measure of the different interest rate environments that then existed, that the World Bank loans were offered to prime borrowers at rates 'as low as 13 per cent', compared to borrowings at more than 17 per cent based on wholesale market rates. The rates for World Bank loans, high though they seem today, were low for that time.

No account of the financial scene of the 1970s would be complete without reference to the activities of the new merchant banking subsidiaries set up by the Bank of Ireland and Allied Irish Banks. These new merchant banks provided formidable competition for each other and of course for ICC's subsidiary Mergers Limited. They were very active in promoting new issues and in the provision of advice on mergers and takeovers. The Investment Bank of Ireland (IBI) was headed up by Charles Rawlinson with the able support of Richard Hooper, while the chief executive of Allied Irish Investment Bank (AIIB) was Martin Rafferty, whose team included Tom Toner and John Hartnett. Both these organisations had the great advantage of access to a huge customer base but that does not in any way detract from the considerable professionalism which they showed in their advisory activities.

Another feature of the 1970s was the development of conglomerates. The first of these appeared when Martin Rafferty and his colleagues left AIIB to use Brooks Thomas as a vehicle for further acquisitions. Soon afterwards Tony O'Reilly, Vincent Ferguson and Nicholas Leonard built up the Fitzwilton conglomerate, using W. & H. M. Goulding as a base. A third venture of this kind was the acquisition of J. Crean & Sons by a group headed by Ray McLoughlin. A feature of all these holding companies was that they were diverse groups very often linked only by common ownership. A main argument in their favour was that their diversity almost guaranteed them against total failure in a period of recession. They were very much in fashion at the time of their inception and have remained in existence, although in some cases the original shareholders are no longer involved.

The Irish National Trading Company (INTC) was formed in 1976 with the objective of making it easier for small companies to export their products. The company's establishment followed a proposal by the Department of Industry and Commerce and Coras Tráchtála Teoranta. It was agreed that ICC would, at its own risk, hold 20 per cent of the equity, the other 80 per cent being held by four leading Irish companies. Because small companies would not have the staff or financial resources to build up significant export contracts, it was felt that INTC would do this and would act as an intermediary for the sale of the goods manufactured by the Irish companies. This initiative proved to be a good example of something that was better in theory than in practice. Very few small companies availed of the new facility and within a few years it was recognised that the concept had not proved acceptable. Accordingly, INTC, which had been launched with a modest fanfare, passed quietly into oblivion. There is no doubt that it was a failure, but if it had not been tried, ICC (and doubtless the other participants) would have regretted their unwillingness to engage in what had seemed like a reasonable venture. One factor which seems to have militated against the success of INTC was a fear felt by some potential exporters that disclosure of their affairs to such a high-powered board might lead to their being swallowed up by one of the large companies represented on that board. Such a fear was probably groundless but business (and other) decisions are often based on perception rather than reality.

By the mid-1970s deposit-taking had become an important part of ICC's financing, representing 20 per cent of its total resources. This was, of course, welcome in that it enabled the company to increase its lending activities.

However, it meant that ICC, the bulk of whose long-term loans had up until then been at fixed rates of interest (thereby removing one element of uncertainty in the generally unpredictable world of business), had to introduce variable-rate lending in respect of a large part of its business. If a financial institution does not 'match' its borrowing and lending terms, it can encounter problems. As deposits were usually on variable terms, logic demanded that a high proportion of the loans made with those deposits should be on related terms. Once again, the importance of the Treasury function in ICC was underlined.

Despite all the problems of the 1970s, ICC was constantly exploring new ways to help trade and industry and new sectors to finance. For example, ICC began to acquire property for lease to industrial and commercial tenants. The first such operation took place in 1976, and the activity was to grow substantially thereafter. By the end of 1979 ICC owned or was committed to nearly eighty industrial and warehouse units. Sale and lease-back terms on existing premises were also introduced, this being a means of providing customers with funds other than by way of loan. While operations of this kind inevitably involved a funding mismatch, the long-term view was taken. Undoubtedly in the early years the rent derived from these premises was not sufficient to cover the interest costs on the monies employed. However, regular rent reviews took place, generally at five-year intervals, and, except in periods of slump, the significant increase in rents following these reviews compensated ICC for its initial financial risk.

One of ICC's main property customers during the late 1970s was the Rohan Group. Ken Rohan, who was chief executive of that group, has made the following comment:

> The financial package agreed with ICC comprised a £750,000 equity injection, giving ICC 22 per cent of the enlarged share capital, and a fixed ten year loan facility at advantageous rates. ICC also agreed to finance the development of up to 200,000 square feet of industrial units over the next five years. This gave Rohan the most important lift-off since the group had become a public company in 1971.

The Rohan Group was just emerging from the very deep recession of 1975-76. The flexibility shown by ICC in understanding our needs at that time was paramount in the massive expansion that our team was able to capitalise on, having negotiated the deal with ICC.

From a shareholders' base of not much more than £1 million in 1978, ICC remained a strategic investor and adviser to Rohan until the company was taken over in September 1987 for £42 million.

There is no doubt in my mind that, without the comprehensive financial package in 1978, which was an enlightened move by ICC at that time in their first major move into investing in a public property company, we would not have achieved the success we managed.

Since its establishment, ICC's specialist property division has been extremely successful in identifying and working with property developers and investors.

In 1976 ICC took a tentative but important step into the growing tourism business. It launched a hotel financing scheme and thereby went against a previous piece of company dogma that tourism was too dangerous a sector for ICC participation. Various prophecies of doom were voiced. Tourism, it was claimed with some validity, was seasonal and much more subject to boom and slump than other trades and industries. Hotels were difficult to run. In any business, the customer must be satisfied but, it was held, in hotels there is no possibility of giving a service that is universally satisfactory. One guest would want silence while another would welcome the omnipresent availability of 'muzak'. Some would require the delights of haute cuisine while others would want quantity rather than quality when ordering food. There would be those who would complain because their room was not ready when they arrived and others who caused this problem by not vacating their rooms on time. And so the catalogue of objections to hotel financing went on.

It was with some trepidation that ICC management proposed to enter this uncharted world of hotel financing, but the board recognised that, from a developmental as well as a commercial point of view, it was a desirable step. Jobs would come on stream much more quickly in the tourist industry than in most other fields of endeavour and there was, of course, a considerable need for new jobs. It was appreciated that hotels need to be professionally managed and ICC decided, not unreasonably, that it would back only hotel projects when there was satisfactory general management experience and capability. The move into hotel financing by ICC proved very successful and it is now one of the largest providers of long-term finance for the Irish hotel industry.

One of ICC's first hotel customers, Charles Sinnott, who is the owner and chief executive of Sinnott Hotels, has given the following view of ICC's involvement in hotel financing:

> Undoubtedly the successful growth of the Irish hotel industry over the past twenty years or so owes much to ICC's identification and special understanding of the sector which, prior to that, had largely been considered an unwelcome risk by the three major lending banks. One suspects and hopes that their courage, at a time when it was deemed neither profitable nor prudent to invest in tourism, has finally paid off as we observe the huge growth in visitor numbers to the country and the success of tourism generally. They certainly deserve much credit for what has been an important role in a national success story. From a personal perspective, I have invariably found ICC very easy to deal with. They seem to have the happy knack of relating well to the smaller operator and so one has always felt more at ease dealing, as it were, with like-minded people who seemed to grasp better the opportunity behind what was, initially at least, a very modest business infrastructure and proposal submitted for funding.

One of ICC's strengths has been derived from the creation of specialist units to deal with specific areas like property, hotels, energy and software. This has enabled ICC to provide an informed service to its customers in those areas.

In 1976 ICC reluctantly accepted that their beautiful Dublin offices in 26 Merrion Square (augmented though they had been by the acquisition of space in Holbrook House, Holles Street) had become too small for a constantly increasing staff. Accordingly, new premises were acquired at 32–34 Harcourt Street. These offices had a Georgian-style frontage, behind which was a modern office block. While Harcourt Street is very different from Merrion Square, it is equally historic. Designed in 1775 by John Hatch, it is a street of great character, where such famous people as Edward Carson, George Bernard Shaw, Cardinal Newman and Bram Stoker have resided. In the past, Harcourt Street was occupied by doctors and lawyers, but today it is a location for commerce and tourism into which ICC has fitted very easily.

The official opening and blessing is believed to have been the first truly ecumenical event of its kind in Ireland as the ceremony involved Christian and Jewish co-operation. Those who took part included Dr Dermot O'Mahony, Roman Catholic Auxiliary Bishop of Dublin; Archdeacon S. G. Poyntz, Church of Ireland; Reverend Dr G. B. McConnell, Presbyterian Church; Reverend Ernest Gallagher, Methodist Church; and Dr Isaac Cohen, Chief Rabbi. Naturally, the quality of the blessing, unique though it was, could not guarantee the continuing adequacy of the new premises for ICC's needs and, in 1979, the current head office, Pinebrook House, which is opposite 32–34 Harcourt Street, was acquired.

ICC financed 1,570 projects in 1979, representing a fourteen-fold growth since the beginning of the decade. By then several loan tranches had been drawn down from the EIB. The total exceeded £60 million, and over 600 projects, mainly for small and medium-sized businesses, had been supported with these EIB monies.

All in all, the 1970s were years of dramatic growth for ICC, notwithstanding the difficulties for the economy created by the oil crises. Advances grew from £4.8 million in 1970 to £66.2 million in 1979, and pre-tax profits from £0.6 million to £3.2 million. There were seventy-seven members of staff in 1970; by 1979 this had increased to 226. The increase in staff led to the gradual disappearance of the family-like intimacy which had characterised ICC in its early years, in favour of a more structured organisation. One of the staff who had lived through both eras commented: 'In the early years, it was very much a family affair. The managing director was the father of the family and a sort of benevolent despot. No one else made decisions, but nevertheless most of the small staff would have gone through fire if asked to do so by the managing director.'

Inevitably something was lost when the company became larger, but there were considerable gains in efficiency. At any rate, the happy atmosphere which was such a feature of ICC continued throughout the 1970s and has done so up to the present day. Kevin O'Connell, who retired in 1992 after twenty years of service, in the course of which he became a general manager, had this to say:

> Having qualified as an engineer, I subsequently became one of UCD's early MBAs. Soon afterwards, I joined ICC where I was immediately impressed by the quality of the staff. It was a great pleasure to work with a team of well-qualified business specialists, with backgrounds in accounting, business studies and finance. I was also struck by the friendly atmosphere which pervaded the office. As ICC was a state-sponsored body, special achievements could not be rewarded tangibly, but one was always praised for a job well done. This was a great motivator and I was glad to be part of such a team. The technician in me was also pleased to be in ICC while it successfully made the transition from operating with simple equipment – when I joined, there was one jealously-guarded calculating machine – to being a completely modern office.

It was natural that, with a much larger staff, there would be greater turnover, particularly as vacancies for experienced people in the expanding financial sector were occurring more frequently. In the early years of ICC, it was viewed as a virtual act of betrayal if any of the team moved elsewhere. The more mature ICC was realistic about mobility. Of course the loss of a member of the team was unwelcome, but there was recognition that movement would occur, both out of and into the company. ICC acquired the reputation of being a training ground for the financial sector.

Pat O'Reilly, a former ICC general manager, went on to become chief executive of the EBS Building Society. Other ICC 'graduates' who are now chief executives of banks include Aidan Brady (Citibank), Colm Darling (ACCBank), Mark Duffy (Bank of Scotland (Ireland)), Ted Marah (Irish Intercontinental Bank), Brian Murphy (ABN AMRO) and Michael Cullen (Investec Gandon). Many others who hold key positions in banks, merchant banks, providers of venture capital and stock-broking firms cut their financial teeth in ICC. Their presence in these other organisations has resulted in much mutual goodwill and valuable contacts. While most of those who have moved have found their niche in the financial world, former ICC personnel are also to be found in other spheres. Examples are Edward Cahill, professor of accountancy at University College, Cork; Damien Kiberd, editor of *The Sunday Business Post*; Maeve Donovan, commercial director of *The Irish Times*; Colum Kelleher, chief executive of the Dakota printing and packaging group; and Barry O'Connor, managing director of McInerney Properties. Cyril McGuire, who is now executive chairman of Trintech Group, speaks as follows about his time in ICC during the 1980s:

My work and responsibilities in ICC gave me a unique exposure to the business dynamics of high-tech industry of both indigenous and overseas companies. This experience has been invaluable to me in Trintech in avoiding some of the common pitfalls associated with building a successful high-tech business. The working environment in ICC rewarded performance and encouraged me to take on additional responsibilities early in my career. This experience of investment appraisal, banking and industry analysis has provided me with a framework to assess commercial opportunities for Trintech in an objective risk/reward perspective.

11

A Lender of Last Resort

Although ICC was a development bank, it was never expected to be a lender of last resort. It would have been impossible for it to discharge such a role and, at the same time, produce annual profits. It did, of course, show more than normal banking patience in dealing with customers in difficulty. Because of the absence of a lender of last resort, ICC often felt it necessary to go somewhat beyond the bounds of prudential lending in order to preserve for a community a business that was in difficulty but which might, with support, find a way out of that difficulty.

A good example of this was the case of Cloth Manufacturers Limited, which was based in Cootehill, County Cavan. The company was set up in the late 1940s to manufacture cloth from reconditioned wool. From the outset it had problems because the first managing director, instead of concentrating on the business for which the company was established, thought he could make a handsome profit by speculating in wool. Having completely misjudged the market and lost most of the company's initial share capital, he left and was replaced by a series of managers from abroad. The frequency of the comings and goings of these managers was such that one local wit remarked on how fortunate it was the factory had two gates – one for outgoing managing directors and the other for those who were replacing them. ICC tried everything to save the company, even at one stage handing over its management to an Italian-led group with considerable experience of manufacturing cloth from reconditioned wool. Despite its expertise, this group failed to achieve success and the only mark it left on the scene was the inclusion of new pasta-based items on the menu of the local hotel. Eventually, after yet another abortive attempt to give it the kiss of life, ICC had to abandon its efforts to save the company.

It was because of experiences like this that in the late 1960s ICC frequently expressed enthusiasm for the idea that a lender of last resort be set up. A development bank like ICC could not ignore the plight of a business in difficulty, but, as it was expected to operate profitably, there was a limit to what it could do to help ailing companies. In 1972 Fóir Teoranta was established. Its objectives and powers were clearly defined in the relevant legislation. Apart from taking over the loans and investments of Táiscí Stáit Teoranta, Fóir could only assist an industrial concern financially if, in the judgement of its board, that concern had, *inter alia*, reasonable prospects of achieving profitability. While it was a lender of last resort, it was not Fóir's function to postpone failure by providing enough money to keep jobs going temporarily. Incidentally, one of its first loans was to Cloth Manufacturers, the company mentioned in the preceding paragraph; unfortunately, the leopard failed to change its spots and eventually the Cootehill company had to be put into receivership.

Throughout its eighteen-year life, Fóir had strong boards which usually included a number of successful businessmen. The chairman of the first board was J. C. B. MacCarthy, former secretary of the Department of Industry and Commerce, and his colleagues were Rory Barnes of Glen Abbey, Eddie Coree of Youghal Carpets, Maurice Cosgrave, a trade unionist, D. D. Coyle of Hygeia Limited, Kevin McCourt, a well-known company director, and Con Murphy, a rights commissioner. J. C. B. MacCarthy was a particularly apt choice for chairman because his years in the Department of Industry and Commerce had given him a comprehensive overview of the industrial scene and its problems. He was an impressive man who bore a striking resemblance to the former British Prime Minister Harold McMillan. While he did not invent the art of delegation, he was assuredly one of its best exponents. The first board was naturally anxious to get its business under way without delay and entered into an agreement with ICC for the provision of management and staff. It was intended that this arrangement would be temporary, ending when Fóir found it possible to recruit its own staff, but the arrangement worked out satisfactorily and continued for ten years. Even when the agreement was ended, most of the staff who had been seconded from ICC remained on as direct employees of Fóir.

Kevin McGuinness, an assistant general manager of ICC, became chief executive of Fóir. He had considerable experience of the problems of industry, having been a civil servant in the Department of Industry and Commerce before joining ICC. The environment in which he and his colleagues found themselves in Fóir was not dissimilar to that which they had left in ICC. The difference was that, whereas in ICC many of the proposals would have had to be regarded as unacceptable, the mandate of Fóir encouraged it to accept a high proportion of them. In its first year alone, Fóir accepted some 70 per cent of the proposals it considered.

The annual reports of Fóir referred in some detail to the types of propositions received. To an ICC ear, they had a disturbingly familiar ring. The main problems affecting the applicant companies were marketing difficulties, under-capitalisation, inadequacy of board and/or management, and amateurish or non-existent costings. Fóir naturally deplored the tendency of so many companies in difficulty to defer making an application until the last minute, normally a sure recipe for disaster but a fault with which anyone involved in banking is all too familiar. In conjunction with other agencies, Fóir made heroic attempts to set up an early warning system and eventually succeeded in doing so. However, the difficulties the would-be customers of Fóir brought with them, particularly those arising from over-borrowing, were often well-nigh incapable of resolution. One of Fóir's problems was that many of those who applied to it saw it as a source of funding and nothing more, whereas Fóir correctly recognised that money was only a part of the solution to most of the difficulties of troubled businesses. To that end, Fóir set up a Management Services Unit. In this unit, Fóir employed consultants who went into companies, advised them and sometimes even managed them. Kevin McGuinness says that, as often as not, the customers were less than profuse in their thanks for non-monetary assistance of this kind.

There were many things which distinguished Fóir from other financial institutions. It did not set out to make a profit, nor could it have done so given the plight of so many of those companies which it financed. While it was able, with considerable justification, to rejoice in its successes, it had to endure a very high incidence of failures. Most organisations welcome repeat business. In Fóir, the sight of an existing customer returning usually meant that more woes were treading on the heels of existing difficulties.

After the retirement of J. C. B. MacCarthy in 1980, Fóir had three further chairmen – Eddie Coree, Noel Hanlon, who later became chairman of Aer Rianta, and Owen Kealy. The following extract from Owen Kealy's statement to Fóir's shareholders sums up his reaction to what he regarded as the unwelcome news of the winding-up of Fóir in 1990, and his assessment of what it had done during its existence:

> There is little left for me to say. Since the demise of Fóir, its loans and investments have been managed for the state by ICC. This is not the place to discuss whether or not Fóir should have been allowed to continue in existence. Suffice it to say that it performed well the job with which it was entrusted and that ICC – in particular those members of its staff who worked in Fóir – can be justifiably proud of having participated in its endeavours.

The decision to end Fóir means that there is now no lender of last resort to which a business in difficulty can turn. However, it can be argued that the economy is mature enough to cope with occasional business failures, and that the existence of strong competition in the banking sector should ensure that a company with reasonable prospects of trading out of its difficulties will be able to obtain financial support. Besides, the kind of financial aid provided by Fóir would inevitably have been under threat from European Union legislation. What is certain is that the activities of Fóir helped to procure the survival of many businesses and the preservation of jobs in the 1970s and 1980s, when unemployment was one of the state's biggest problems.

12

Who Told the Chairman it was Tuesday?

The year 1972 was a special milestone in ICC's history because it marked Dr J. P. Beddy's retirement. He had served with ICC for thirty-nine years, firstly as secretary, then, having spent a brief period as a non-executive director, as chairman and managing director, and finally as ICC's first non-executive chairman. No memoir of ICC and its development would be complete without a special reference to Dr Beddy. He was educated at O'Connell Schools, where he was a contemporary and friend of Seán Lemass. He was an inspector of taxes before joining ICC as secretary. He had spent most of his early working life in Kerry and he jokingly claimed that, when he left Kerry, there was substantially less money in circulation there than before he arrived. He was very fond of Kerry and enjoyed his negotiations with the reluctant but charming taxpayers of that county, some of whom euphemistically referred to their efforts to deceive him as 'little bits of strategy'. So much did Kerry mean to him that he often said that his time in that county had been the happiest period of his private life. His part in ICC's development was considerable. In the early years he took to the public issue life like a duck to water and, when the emphasis shifted from share flotations to other forms of financing, he played a major part in ICC's subsequent progress and adaptations.

Many tributes have been paid to Beddy, the most notable being that written by Dr Whitaker (see Appendix 2). It is, therefore, unnecessary to go into detail about his academic accomplishments, his total dedication to work as evidenced by his competent direction of three state-sponsored bodies simultaneously, and his complete integrity. It is probably not generally known that he was one of a small group of businessmen whose deliberations led to the founding of the Irish Management Institute. What is even less well known about him is that he had a keen sense of humour and an ability to create a complete word picture in a single sentence. To most of those who met him, Beddy was an austere man who took everything seriously. They would have been surprised to know that, in the presence of his friends, he often presented a totally different image. This chapter contains a few examples of the side of Beddy which was less well known to the public.

A friend of his acquired a cottage in a rural setting and invited Beddy to visit it. When he returned, he was asked what the cottage was like. He replied, 'It's a place with hens outside the door', and one could immediately almost see, smell and feel the place so economically described.

Sometimes, if he was having lunch at a distance from the office, he would take a lift from one of the staff. On one occasion his driver was Larry Tuomey, who is now a director of the Cross Group. Tuomey recalls that he had just acquired a new car which was painted in an extremely bright shade of turquoise. His pride in his car was somewhat tempered (but, happily, not completely obliterated) when Beddy dryly observed: 'I suppose you had to take whatever colour they offered you'.

Having worked hard for his own degrees, Beddy had a great respect for university education and was always predisposed to admitting to the staff someone with a good academic record. This resulted in ICC having a staff of very high intellectual calibre, but it may also have led to the belief that a university education was almost an essential pre-requisite for employment there. One former employee of ICC was asked by a junior member of staff in his new place of work whether there were any job prospects in ICC. He was informed solemnly, but mendaciously, that he would have no hope of success unless he had a university degree.

Beddy did not approve of heavy drinkers and gamblers. He had a keen nose and, if a would-be customer displayed signs of over-indulgence in alcohol, his chances of success were very limited. It is doubtful if Beddy himself ever entered a public house. On one occasion he was considerably distressed when, on leaving a restaurant in a hotel, he met some of the university students to whom he lectured. As the restaurant and bar were close together, he was worried lest they might think he had been imbibing. He could well have reflected that, however censorious students might have been in other respects, it was very unlikely that the consumption of alcohol would have figured on their list of the seven deadly sins.

One of the more extraordinary applications for a loan came from someone who proposed setting up a maggotorium which, as its name implies, was to produce maggots for sale to fishermen. The submission made it clear that the maggotorium building and its surroundings would be extremely malodorous. With characteristic wit, Beddy wrote on the relevant report: 'Count me out for the official opening'.

One morning Beddy met a young member of the staff on the way into the office and enquired what day of the week it was. He was told it was Tuesday. On reaching his desk, he discovered from the calendar that it was Wednesday. He casually mentioned the episode to Connor, the company secretary. Every remark by Beddy, however trivial, was treated seriously by Connor. An astounded Beddy later found that a solemn enquiry had been instituted to find out who had told the chairman it was Tuesday!

In the limited spare time which he had available, Beddy's favourite leisure activities were reading (mostly biographies) and listening to operatic and orchestral music. One learns from Leon Ó Broin's book *No Man's Man* that, during the centenary celebrations of the Statistical and Social Inquiry Society of Ireland, Beddy and Joe Brennan, then governor of the Central Bank, missed a performance of Scriabin's 'Le Poème de l'Extase' in order to walk in the grounds of Trinity College, Dublin, and have a conversation about economic matters. Those who do not admire Scriabin's music would, no doubt, regard this event as confirming the high quality of Beddy's taste in music. He was not a regular theatre-goer, but he enjoyed some of the Abbey productions and he often quoted approvingly the line in O'Casey's *The Plough and the Stars* when Fluther observed: 'I wasn't goin' to let meself be malignified by a chancer'. His affection for this line may have sprung from his own career as an inspector of taxes, when the spotting of 'chancers' came as second nature to him. This talent was also all-important in ICC, particularly in the early days, in dealing with the many dubious applicants who looked for financial support.

Beddy was one of a particular brand of patriotic Irishmen who flourished during the early years of the state. They were to be found in politics, in the civil service, in the professions and in business. Their primary motivation was not the acquisition of personal wealth but the desire to do a good job for the community. Two of Beddy's contemporaries in state-sponsored bodies also come to mind in this context – Jerry Dempsey who, after a short while in industry, spent most of his life as chief executive of Aer Lingus, and Todd Andrews, who devoted himself to building up another state-sponsored body, Bord na Móna. In the civil service there were many dedicated people, such as Joe Brennan and J. J. McElligott and later Dr T. K. Whitaker, who left an indelible mark on the Department of Finance. Without their contribution and that of many other giants, it is unlikely that the Ireland of today would have achieved its current prosperity.

Beddy remained keenly interested in ICC's activities until his death in 1976. Despite his many successes in other fields, it can be said with certainty that ICC was the organisation that was dearest to his heart. He was proud of its achievements. During his time as chairman and chief executive ICC expanded into several new areas. He would undoubtedly have welcomed the considerable diversification and growth which has occurred in ICC during the past quarter century.

13

Four Chairmen in Ten Years

In its first thirty-nine years ICC had only two chairmen – J. P. Colbert and J. P. Beddy. By contrast, the 1970s proved to be the decade of four chairmen.

When Beddy retired in 1972, he was succeeded as chairman by Denis Herlihy, managing director of the Insurance Corporation of Ireland. Herlihy, who was already a board member, had been a senior civil servant before being recruited by the insurance world and, during his time in office, the company for which he was responsible showed impressive growth. Beddy had been a non-executive chairman for his final three years in office, but Herlihy was the first ICC chairman who had not previously held an executive position in the company. His successors have also been non-executive. In line with best modern practice, the roles of chairman and chief executive have been separate in ICC for more than thirty years.

Although Herlihy's period of office was short (he died in 1976), his contribution was valuable. Because he had not grown up in the company, he brought a greater objectivity to the job than would have been possible if he had been appointed from within. Although somewhat brusque in manner and often hasty in reaching conclusions, he had a great understanding of the problems of running a business and was always prepared to listen to and act upon reasoned argument. Being a managing director himself, he understood that the primary job of a board is to decide on policy and strategy, leaving the implementation task to management. Although completely different to Beddy in manner and outlook, he possessed, like his predecessor, the great virtue of integrity. Before going into business, he worked in the Department of Industry and Commerce. During the war years, he was assigned to the Department of Supplies, where he may have acquired one of his pet obsessions – economising on the use of paper by writing on both sides of the sheet. He had a deep commitment to the country and its institutions, a commitment which he brought in full measure to his chairmanship of ICC.

When Denis Herlihy died, one of the other members of the board, James T. Barton, succeeded him. Jim Barton was to be chairman twice, firstly for two years from 1977 to 1979 and then from 1984 to 1992. He is a distinguished former president of the Society of the Irish Motor Industry and, indeed, is one of the few people to have held that office on two occasions. As in Herlihy's case, he brought something new to the job of chairman, understanding fully the need for the separation of functions between non-executive directors and management. Unlike Herlihy, however, his manner has always been anything but brusque and as chairman he was admired for his courtesy and deep concern, not only for ICC's customers, but also for the management and staff. He admits to having had no background in banking, but he proved to be a quick learner and, while totally committed to discharging a non-executive role, he readily passed on the benefits of his experience as a businessman. While he is a racing aficionado, he is by no means an indiscriminate gambler. As chairman of ICC, he recognised that a balance had to be struck between a prudent approach to banking and a realisation that an organisation like ICC can only achieve growth if it is prepared to take reasonable risks.

J. G. (Gerry) Hickey was chairman from 1979 to 1984. He is a well-known Dublin solicitor and a former president of the Law Society. He is also an experienced businessman who has served on many boards. One of his early statements as chairman drew attention to a problem which was not confined to ICC but which, nevertheless, hampered its ability to retain staff. He pointed out that ICC, being largely state-owned, was treated as part of the public sector even though it was in competition with a host of financial institutions in the private sector, which rewarded their staff more favourably. He added:

> My colleagues and I view with concern what seems to us to be an over-rigid interpretation in some quarters of the principle of the unity of the Public Service. We recognise that being part of the Public Service imposes certain disciplines on an organisation and we do not object to such disciplines provided they are applied with flexibility.

The wisdom of these observations is borne out by the flexible arrangements subsequently made for several commercial state-sponsored bodies.

14

Professionals, Nominees and Others

Like any other financial institution, ICC deals with professional people, particularly the accountants who submit propositions on behalf of their clients, and also their clients' solicitors, architects and engineers. For the most part, these encounters have been entirely satisfactory. Indeed, from ICC's point of view, the presence of a competent accountant is often reassuring because such an adviser would be unlikely to submit a proposition in which he or she had no confidence. Apart from their principal role as advisers to their clients, professional people were sometimes asked by ICC to act as their nominees on the boards of companies to which ICC had advanced funds.

One of these professionals became chairman of a company which had been the subject of a flotation underwritten by ICC. Today's captains of industry, who hire public relations consultants to ensure high-quality publicity for their meetings of shareholders, would have been horrified if they had been present at the annual general meetings of the company concerned. One year the secretary of the company had (unwisely as it turned out) informed the press that the annual general meeting would be at a certain time and place. Obligingly, reporters and photographers turned up, but their stay was short lived. Far from welcoming them, the chairman wanted to know who had allowed these people into the room and refused to proceed with the meeting until they and their equipment had been removed. As the company was struggling at the time to gain home market share against competitive imports, one can readily understand why it continued to struggle and ultimately collapsed.

It must be emphasised that this is a very unusual tale. Most of ICC's contacts with professional people were entirely satisfactory. Probably the outstanding professionals dealt with during ICC's early years were Vincent Crowley, accountant, and Arthur Cox, solicitor. Vincent Crowley was founder of Kennedy Crowley & Company, a firm which grew organically and by mergers over the years and is now KPMG in Ireland. Arthur Cox was the founder and managing partner of the legal firm which still bears his name. While their firms were not formally linked, they often worked together on projects and were a formidable pair. It is hard to imagine two more dissimilar people, although they were good friends and went to Lourdes together every year to act as brancardiers. Crowley dressed well, presented his case in a structured way and put everything important in writing. Cox was a brilliant eccentric, who consistently managed to wear his tie inside out and wore a battered hat and a raincoat which had seen better days. He appeared to be totally disorganised but his considerable intellectual powers were evident when he tendered his advice.

Vincent Crowley's sons followed in their father's footsteps and had many dealings with ICC on behalf of their clients. The eldest, Niall, who died in 1998, was the first managing partner of Stokes Kennedy Crowley (initially a combination of Kennedy Crowley & Company and Stokes Brothers & Pim). He inherited his father's accounting ability, and his work as receiver for ICC in some difficult cases was carried out with professionalism and flair. He later became chairman of Allied Irish Banks.

Another group of advisers who were very important to ICC, especially when it was heavily involved in public flotations, were stockbrokers. The first brokers appointed to assist ICC were Butler & Briscoe and O'Brien & Toole. When a vital decision on the issue price of shares had to be made, several earnest sessions were held with Desmond Butler, Brendan Briscoe and Esmonde O'Brien, or in later years with Ken Beaton and Colm O'Briain. Although ICC's own stockbrokers were those most frequently consulted, there were also discussions with other firms, such as Davy Stockbrokers, who were acting for the companies whose shares were being floated. Brokers have not always enjoyed all the back-up services which are available to stockbroking firms today. Nevertheless, although they sometimes gave the impression that their views were based on little more than a hunch, their advice was almost invariably sound. A welcome feature of ICC's annual general meetings has always been the attendance, as shareholders, of several stockbrokers.

A list of all the accountants, solicitors and other professionals with whom ICC has had dealings would inevitably result in some inadvertent omissions. Reference must be made, however, to ICC's first external auditor, Dermot Shortall, who was regarded with a mixture of awe and affection by the staff. At that time Shortall was exercising a dual mandate. In addition to his main work in Kevans & Son, he was also a sort of regent in the firm of Gardner Donnelly. The managing partner of that concern had died unexpectedly at an early age and his son, John Donnelly, was too young to take over the reins of office. Consequently, Shortall discharged the role of managing partner until John was experienced enough to succeed him. Following several mergers, Gardner Donnelly became part of Deloitte & Touche, of which John Donnelly was the first chairman. Donnelly was admired in ICC for his decisive approach to problems. In one of his receiverships, he found it necessary to change all the locks in a factory at very short notice because he had reason to believe that the proprietors were planning to remove the stocks, which were very mobile, in advance of the receivership becoming effective. He confesses that his most frightening moment was when, in another case, he had to go a long way underground to inform 160 understandably aggrieved colliery workers that they were redundant.

Reverting to ICC's own auditors, Kevans & Son (one of several firms which made up Coopers & Lybrand, which is now part of PricewaterhouseCoopers), Dermot Shortall's son Paddy had responsibility for the ICC audit for several years. Other partners in that firm who have dealt with ICC include John Mahon, Kevin Kelly (now managing director, Allied

Irish Banks) and Bill Cunningham. Happily, all of them in their time had no difficulty in confirming, in the well-turned phraseology of the accounting profession, that the accounts of ICC gave a true and fair view of the state of the company's affairs.

15

The Beginning of the Transformation:
The Eighties

The economic climate was difficult in the early 1980s. Interest and inflation rates were at high levels, with money market rates and inflation exceeding 20 per cent at times. For companies importing or exporting, currency fluctuations sometimes had dramatic effects. Other rising domestic costs made it difficult for Irish industry to remain competitive and there was a high level of business failure. Heavy budget deficits were incurred by the state and painful remedial action had to be taken.

Politically the 1980s began with what might be described as a series of 'revolving door' governments. At the outset there was the Fianna Fáil government which had been elected in 1977. Then several elections took place and each time there was a change of government. The period up to and following the general election of 1987 continued to be marked by great economic difficulty and financial stringency. To quote Dermot McAleese: 'By that time, every canon of macro-stability had been spectacularly breached and the Irish economy had come close to financial disaster' (1997/8: p.8). The new Fianna Fáil government was generally supported by the Fine Gael opposition in taking a firm line about the economy – Alan Dukes, then leader of Fine Gael, had put forward this policy in his 'Tallaght Strategy' speech. In 1989 yet another election led to a Fianna Fáil/Progressive Democrats government.

ICC had to operate in a difficult environment characterised by weak investment, particularly in the early years of the decade. Nevertheless, ICC continued to expand its existing facilities and broadened the range of its services into strongly commercial areas such as foreign exchange, international asset financing, and international trade services. In 1980 its total assets were £216 million. By 1990 this figure had grown to more than £1 billion.

During the late 1970s and throughout the 1980s ICC provided financial assistance for many industries which, in the difficult prevailing market conditions, were in a very fragile state. Kingspan Group plc is a good example of the kind of support provided by ICC. The subsequent positive impact that this support had on employment in the Cavan/Monaghan region, and on the balance of payments because of substantial exports, was a source of satisfaction to both Kingspan and ICC.

The Kingspan Group had been established in the 1970s by two brothers, Gene and Brendan Murtagh. Gene Murtagh made the following comment:

> In 1979, while Kingspan was in the early stages of developing the composite panel business for which it has become well known, ICC provided a loan and equity package, subscribing for 19 per cent of the issued share capital. In 1982 Kingspan encountered difficult market conditions in all its markets, and the problem was compounded when a major overseas contract could not be completed because the customer could not comply with the terms of the contract. There is no doubt that, were it not for the support provided by ICC, Kingspan would not have survived this period and would not have gone on to become one of the most successful growth companies listed on the Irish Stock Exchange.

During the 1980s deposits became the single largest source of funds for ICC as the tap of exchequer advances was turned off, in part because of a general cut-back in government expenditure, and was replaced by a repayment schedule for those advances. The World Bank loans were repaid and ICC's requests for finance from the European Investment Bank were relatively modest. The international funding base was extended in 1986 when ICC was the first non-sovereign Irish borrower to arrange a Euro Commercial Paper Program, the amount involved being US$ 100 million.

For ICC the 1980s were a divided period. During the first half of the decade, ICC implemented several concessionary funding schemes on behalf of the state. For much of that period Irish interest rates were considerably higher than other European rates. For example, Irish short-term rates averaged about 12 per cent in the 1980s, whereas the corresponding German average rate was 6.5 per cent. ICC, with government help, was able to provide funds for industry at rates comparable to those available to its competitors in the European Economic Community. However, by the mid-1980s, ICC's developmental role was becoming less important and the various support schemes which it operated were phased out.

Not all of ICC's new endeavours were successful. One which had an unsatisfactory outcome was the establishment of a new subsidiary, ICC Fund Management Limited. The objective of this company was to provide fund management services for pension funds, corporate funds, private client portfolios and religious bodies and charities. Research had indicated that, with ICC's substantial customer base, this could be a fruitful source of business. In the event, however, customers proved to be very slow to move their fund management to a completely new operator and, by the end of the 1980s, it became clear that a relatively small player like ICC, even though it managed competently and successfully the funds entrusted to it, could not compete effectively in that market.

A more successful area for ICC has been international consulting. For many years ICC was used by the World Bank as a role model for other development finance institutions, because it had managed to combine development banking with profitability. It occasionally carried out advisory assignments for individual companies. Arising from this experience, in 1989 ICC combined with the Industrial Development Authority, Coras Tráchtála Teoranta, Shannon Development and Coillte Teoranta to develop a commercial international consultancy business through a new company –

International Development Ireland Limited (IDI). The objective of IDI was to use the expertise of its constituent organisations to provide much-needed advice in developing countries.

With the board and staff drawn from the five organisations and an independent chairman, IDI got under way and operated successfully for many years. Various consultancy assignments were commissioned by the World Bank and also by individual governments. When communism collapsed in eastern Europe, the European Union set up two technical assistance programmes and IDI obtained many assignments under those programmes.

One problem, however, was that not all the participating organisations were of the same mind, and eventually cracks in the edifice began to appear. Accordingly, in 1997 IDI was sold to another international consulting group. However, the individual organisations remained free to offer consultancy services in their own areas of expertise, and ICC is still active in providing such services through ICC Consulting. It has carried out advisory work in central and eastern Europe, the Far East, South America and several African countries. This activity is profitable in itself and has done a great deal to help financial and other organisations in the countries concerned. Projects currently being undertaken include the provision of training to the Czech financial sector on European Monetary Union and preparation for accession to the European Union. ICC Consulting is helping to develop the Environmental Investment Fund in Latvia. Members of ICC staff are managing the Guyana National Co-operative Bank, and setting a new strategic direction.

The experience has not been without its moments to remember. In one African bank, where ICC provided advice, it transpired that more than 90 per cent of the bank's loans were non-earning. To drag such an institution back from the realm of insolvency was a task beyond the capacity of even the cleverest banker. In an agriculturally-based African development bank, which ICC consultants were managing, an ICC executive found to his astonishment that one of his duties involved the corralling of cattle. Another member of the ICC team was asked to receive a letter of protest from customers of the bank who feared its closure. He found himself at the front door facing about 750 locals who were engaged in a very lively native 'dance', which was normally a prelude to battle. Fortunately, the ritual, although serious, was intended as no more than a demonstration of discontent and did not involve a physical threat.

Reverting to the early 1980s, one of the most significant events affecting industry was the commissioning by the National Economic and Social Council of a report on industrial strategy. This report, which became known as the Telesis Report, after the name of the American organisation which carried it out, was published in 1982. It contained detailed analysis and criticism of past and present industrial policies and included several hard-hitting but positive recommendations. Telesis was generous in its tributes to the way in which state-sponsored bodies concerned with industries were run, but was less complimentary when it reflected on the degree to which Irish industrial policy goals had been achieved. It found that:

- high skilled, high technology industries were rare;
- Irish indigenous exports were small and limited geographically;
- Irish companies were not providing sub-supplies to foreign-owned industry;
- small firms were generally low skilled;
- there was little co-operation between primary producers and processors in raw material based businesses;
- foreign-owned industry was often unsophisticated, with little prospect of substantial improvement.

There was a rap on the knuckles for those who believed that the way forward for Irish industry was to bring in more foreign-owned industries without devoting any serious attention to indigenous industries. By their nature, the report contended, these domestically-owned industries would be less mobile than those whose owners lived abroad. Some of the findings of the Telesis Report proved to be unduly pessimistic, but it served the purpose of causing the various agencies concerned with industrial development to examine what they were doing and to make important changes. Telesis took a fairly benign view of ICC because its broadly commercial outlook was accompanied by a concern for matters like employment potential and regional development.

In the early 1980s ICC was still wearing its developmental hat and, following the Minister for Finance's budget of 1982, two new ICC loans were introduced – the Working Capital Loan Scheme and Working Capital for Exports. These loan schemes allowed Irish businesses to obtain working capital finance at interest rates closely related to those which applied in the continental export markets where they were competing. The schemes were availed of by some 700 manufacturers. At about this time ICC was increasingly conscious of the difficulties involved in trying to ride two horses at the same time. On the one hand, there was the activity of a development bank, and on the other a commercial function. The chairman at the 1982 annual general meeting emphasised this by saying that ICC's objective was 'to contribute to national development by providing capital, including venture capital, to the business sector while, at the same time, operating profitably'.

ICC celebrated its golden jubilee in 1983. The government marked the occasion by increasing the number of directors from seven to nine and by putting an official of the Department of Finance on the board, this after fifty years when there had been no such direct representation. It would be an exaggeration to describe the reaction of the board and management of ICC to this development as one of jubilation. Relations with the Department of Finance were good and had been so for many years. The board could see no justification for the department having, as they saw it, a spy in the cab. They believed that conflicts of interest would arise frequently for the department representative, and they also feared that the person appointed would act as a brake on progress. One of them recalled having visited the Department of Industry and Commerce with an industrialist who paused on the steps to say: 'Welcome to the world of commercial unreality'.

The fears expressed by the board proved to be exaggerated. The first official appointed, Michael Neville, was an able director who helped to simplify contacts with the Department of Finance. His successors, Phelim Molloy, Tom Considine, David Doyle, and Donal McNally, have all done likewise. This is not the place to argue the case for or against direct departmental representation on boards of state-sponsored bodies, but the experience of ICC indicates that, if there must be such representation, the Department of Finance is able to nominate people of excellent quality to act on its behalf. Reference has earlier been made to the helpful attitude taken towards ICC by Dr Whitaker. This has also applied to his successors – C. H. Murray, Michael Murphy, Tomás Ó Cofaigh, Maurice Doyle, Seán Cromien, Paddy Mullarkey and the current Secretary General, John Hurley.

The Industrial Credit (Amendment) Act of 1983 doubled ICC's borrowing powers to £800 million, a sign of the rapid growth which the company was experiencing. The company, while still discharging a developmental role, was at the same time aiming to achieve full commercial profitability. ICC, even at its most developmental, was always anxious to avoid supporting the setting up of an industry or business which was likely to be short-lived. The immediate benefit conferred on a community by the additional spending power generated by increased employment is more than off-set by the heartache and disappointment which follow the closure of a business.

Offshore oil exploration was one of the flavours of the year in 1983 and ICC, through ICC Corporate Finance Limited, took an active role in this area. The search for oil off the Irish coast was unashamedly speculative. If any of the original directors of ICC had still been around, they would undoubtedly have criticised the company for associating itself with what might have been perceived as little more than gambles – even if the gamblers wore Armani shirts and Gucci ties! However, on reflection, they might have also drawn a parallel between oil exploration and their own pioneering work with green-field enterprises in the 1930s.

In the early 1980s there was still a reluctance on the part of private individuals to commit funds to equity in private companies. This prompted ICC's chairman, Gerry Hickey, to make the following suggestion in his 1983 chairman's statement: 'We believe that some form of tax incentive ... for all equity investments up to, say, £25,000 would greatly encourage private investors'. His suggestion, although not acted upon immediately, would find substantial acceptance in the following year.

In 1984 James T. Barton became chairman again. One of the first things he did was welcome to the board Pádraic White, managing director of the Industrial Development Authority (IDA). That appointment was part of a reciprocal arrangement (long since abandoned) whereby the managing directors of ICC and the IDA were each members of the other's board. The idea behind this arrangement was good. The two organisations had very different functions, but they both had a special interest in industrial development, an interest which was helped by closer cooperation between them.

There had been no increase in share capital since 1962 and ICC's capital adequacy ratio was unsatisfactory. Accordingly, there was a welcome in 1986 for the subscription by the Minister for Finance of further shares to increase the issued capital from £8.8 million to £12 million. There was now a definite recognition of the fact that ICC's developmental role was being phased out and that a movement towards a widened and more commercial role was gathering momentum. Jim Barton, in his statement to the annual general meeting in that year, said: 'Many of ICC's activities are controlled by legislation which was enacted more than 50 years ago. ... ICC has sought amendments to its legislation which would have the effect of enabling it to operate in new and growing sectors of business and to provide additional financial services'.

An event of major significance occurred in 1987. The International Financial Services Centre (IFSC), the brainchild of Dermot Desmond, was set up in Dublin – a most imaginative development which has proved extremely successful. ICC's subsidiary, ICC International Finance Limited, obtained a licence to operate in the IFSC, carrying out international asset financing transactions. The centre has expanded rapidly and, at the time of writing, there are about 400 international institutions operating from IFSC. Practically all the household names in the financial world are there – Citibank, Merrill Lynch, Deutsche Morgan Grenfell, Société Générale, Mitsubishi Bank, NatWest and ABN AMRO, to name only a few. There are attractive tax and other concessions available to those who set up an operation in the IFSC. Incidentally, the success of the Dublin IFSC has been helpful in enabling ICC Consulting to negotiate a contract with the government of Botswana. Under that contract, an IFSC has been established in that country and ICC Consulting advised on the tax, legislative and regulatory environment in which it operates.

When the government took steps to control the exchequer deficit in 1987, this was welcomed by ICC, particularly as a reduction in interest rates ensued. In the following year, the company achieved new banking records, with its loan portfolio growing by 20 per cent to £470 million. The company's equity investments were also showing considerable growth, not all of which was reflected in the annual accounts. ICC Corporate Finance Limited was particularly busy in 1988 because, apart from being heavily involved in ICC's subscriptions for shares, it sponsored two flotations and broadened the scope of its advisory activities to include overseas transactions, management buy-outs, company disposals and strategic planning.

Encouraged by the success of its first branch office in Cork, ICC had set up an office in Limerick in 1974 and its business in the mid-west area had grown steadily. By 1989 the expansion had reached such a level that a move to larger premises was essential. Accordingly, ICC's Limerick operation was moved to new headquarters, which it continues to occupy at ICC House, Charlotte Quay.

As the 1990s approached, the transformation of ICC had begun. The line from Macbeth, 'If it were done when 'tis done, then 'twere well it were done quickly', may well have been in the minds of ICC personnel but, realistically, it had to be accepted that a rapid change in the status of a state-sponsored organisation was unlikely. Nevertheless, change was on the way and would occur dramatically during the following decade.

16

The Business Expansion Scheme –
Its Rise and Fall

One of the areas in which ICC has been pre-eminent is the Business Expansion Scheme (BES). This chapter attempts to describe the rapid progress of the BES and how, like Humpty Dumpty, it had such a great fall that a large part of it could not be put together again.

The Finance Act of 1984 introduced a tax concession designed to encourage individuals to invest in private Irish companies, particularly manufacturing companies, over a period of at least five years. Individuals making such investments were allowed to write off the amount subscribed against their top rate of income tax. Traditionally, Irish people had been very reluctant to invest in private companies. The BES sought to remedy this and thereby increase the supply of capital to Irish business from private investment rather than from dependence on debt.

Attractive though the tax concession was, it was difficult for individuals to identify and evaluate private companies in which they might invest. Consequently the practice of setting up BES funds was begun. These funds were run by people and financial institutions experienced in business banking and finance and enabled individual investors to leave risk assessment to the experts and, at the same time, spread their risk over several companies. ICC launched its first BES fund in 1990. One would like to be able to say that it took the world by storm, but sadly this was not so. A target of £2 million was set but, modest though the objective was, it erred on the side of over-optimism and only £1.1 million was raised.

Undaunted by this early setback, ICC saw the potential for BES funds and a separate team was set up to identify suitable companies for investment. In the following year the ICC BES Tourism Fund was launched. This could be described as the first 'themed' fund in Ireland, as it set out to raise funds for investment in hotels and tourism-related businesses. ICC, as we have seen, has played a strong part in the development of the sector. It was the first Irish bank with a dedicated hotels division and it felt reasonably confident of raising a £6 million fund. This proved to be a conservative estimate; the demand from subscribers would almost have been sufficient to double the targeted amount, but eventually ICC settled for £8 million. The success was remarkable, especially as the government, shortly after the launch of the fund, announced, through the budget speech of the Minister for Finance, the exclusion of hotels from the BES and the reduction of the maximum which could be invested in any one company from £2.5 million to £500,000. With the help of some transitional arrangements agreed with the Department of Finance, ICC managed, in the very short time permitted, to make investments in ten tourism projects. Hotels and other tourism facilities were improved considerably by the BES and it is encouraging that there has been an unprecedented growth in tourist numbers since the mid-1990s.

With hotels excluded from the BES, ICC went back to its first love – manufacturing industry. In the next three years it raised a total of £13 million. In each of those years, the ICC BES fund was heavily over-subscribed; it was the largest fund in the market and it was the first fund to be closed. It was not surprising that the 1995 fund, which had an initial target of £5 million, was closed at £8.5 million within a few days of opening. The demand was so great (one investor threatened legal proceedings if his money was not accepted), that a second fund to raise a further £5 million was immediately opened.

ICC was now experiencing the consequences of success. An unlimited BES fund was not feasible because monies had to be invested within one year, there was a limited pool of acceptable quality investments, and the work of assessing and processing potential investments absorbed a good deal of staff resources; on average over the period, only one out of every three investments assessed was made. It was decided that, in the interests of having a more orderly procedure, existing investors would be given advance notice of the opening of the 1996 BES fund. Again, ICC found itself discharging a task not dissimilar to that of the sorcerer's apprentice; the fund had to be closed at £8.1 million and could not be opened to the public generally. In 1997 part of the BES fund was reserved for first-time investors, but queues formed hours before the offices opened and the fund was closed on the day of the launch. ICC may have had to struggle to obtain investors in 1990, but seven years later it was the investors who struggled to gain access to ICC's BES fund.

It was not known at the time, but the 1997 BES fund was to mark the end of the heady days of BES. Throughout the 1990s the government had carried out a number of fine-tuning exercises designed to eliminate abuses. For instance, when the BES was introduced, it was possible through the use of bank guarantees to make the investment nearly risk-free. Since the tax concession was designed to be a reward for risk, this anomaly was stamped out. It was also provided that there should be certification of employment-creation potential. Unless, like the leprechaun's pot of gold, there was the prospect of creating or saving jobs at the end of the rainbow, a company would not qualify for BES monies.

Some of the changes were necessary. Others fell into the category of irritants, which made BES an over-complicated product. In the eyes of BES fund managers, however, all this paled into insignificance beside the provision in the 1997 budget, which limited the maximum amount to be invested in any one company to £250,000. Some BES fund managers made angry noises. Others protested silently by withdrawing from the market. ICC, although upset by this new provision, decided, as market leader, to launch a BES fund in 1998 to test how it would operate despite the new restrictions. The launch was successful in itself. The target, a relatively modest

£3 million, was reached easily and the fund was closed within an hour of opening. It was then satisfactorily invested. However, it was to be ICC's last BES fund. Even a relatively small fund like £3 million meant that twelve suitable companies for investment had to be found, assessed and monitored for at least the next five years. This made the BES uneconomic and unattractive for ICC.

The effective demise of BES fund operations is a matter for regret. ICC alone raised £55 million in nine years and invested in seventy-six companies. The typical investee company was a small or medium-sized business with an expansion programme. It was generally under-capitalised and over-dependent on debt. The BES investments strengthened the balance sheets of such companies. They even helped some companies to survive the currency crisis of 1992/3, when short-term interest rates averaged around 35 per cent per annum and were often at even more prohibitively high levels. While no total figures for BES job-creation are available, estimates prepared in 1995 by four BES fund managers (including ICC) showed that, at that stage, £42 million of BES investments had resulted in almost 1,500 new jobs in sixty-eight companies.

One recurring criticism of the BES was that it helped 'fat cat' investors to grow fatter by shielding them from their tax burden. Nothing could have been further from the truth. ICC's experience with more than 3,000 investors shows that, while there were some individuals who invested the maximum of £25,000 in each year, the overall average investment was less than £10,000. Indeed, more than half of the investors subscribed £5,000 or less. These small investors can hardly be accused of trying to scoop the pot, although their flirtation with risk has, so far, worked out well since the ICC BES funds realised so far have given investors satisfactory annual returns.

Companies now need to have a minimum valuation exceeding £200 million to make it worth their while to seek a stock market quotation. Thus, the average individual at present has little opportunity, other than that presented by the occasional privatisation of state-sponsored companies, to invest in Irish companies. Perhaps early in this century there will be a return to more realistic BES investment limits, and the sun will again shine on small and medium-sized industry, to say nothing of the small-scale investor seeking a modest and legitimate tax reduction in return for the acceptance of risk.

17

Some Lost – and Found – Causes

Every bank receives unusual propositions. From its earliest days ICC was the recipient of such projects. They included improbable proposals such as a scheme to anchor floating islands in the Atlantic, and the manufacture of a briefcase that would automatically play music when it was unlocked.

On one occasion ICC was visited by a group of Chicago businessmen, who had what was regarded in those days as an outlandish proposal to establish gambling dens all over the city of Dublin and, in due course, the rest of the country. They had brought with them a priest from the Chicago diocese. Clearly they felt that in Holy Ireland the presence of a clergyman would lend respectability to an otherwise dubious proposal. Perhaps they had in mind Shakespeare's lines: 'What damned error but some sober brow will bless it and approve it with a text hiding the grossness with fair ornament'. Leo Conway, who was the ICC official dealing with them, averred that he had seen a hearse parked outside the front door and that one of the group had left a violin case for safe keeping at the reception desk. Although this was an amusing flight of fancy, one would not have been surprised to find that, at some stage in their lives, the group might have been called upon to help the Chicago police with their enquiries.

Despite the occasional bizarre project, most submissions to ICC have been concerned with sensible and well-researched proposals. Even some propositions which, when presented, seemed to be 'such stuff as dreams are made on', proved to be well founded. For example, Roger Johnson had been engaged in mining in Africa and when he came to Ireland believed that with proper development the Aillwee Cave in County Clare, then little more than a hole in the earth, could become a commercial success. ICC backed the proposal and, after much expenditure on exploration and development, it proved to be the realisation of Roger Johnson's dream. Today it is Ireland's premier show-cave. Johnson's accountant remarked when the ICC loan was approved: 'I don't know anyone else who would give us money for a hole in the ground'.

Although ICC has had only limited resources available for sponsorship, its selective support has had considerable long-term benefits for the world of music. Judith Woodworth, director of the National Concert Hall, told how it happened:

> I would not have been able to bring such distinguished artists as Anne-Sophie Mütter to Ireland without financial support. At the time I had begun to organise celebrity concerts at the National Concert Hall but I did not have financial backing. I had recently returned to work in Dublin, having been involved in concert promotion in London for several years. The ready and enthusiastic response which ICC gave to my request for assistance was both gratifying and encouraging. Following the success of these opening concerts, the Celebrity Concert Series has become one of the most successful annual events of the National Concert Hall's calendar.

A chapter concerned with diverse events is an appropriate place in which to refer with pride to the only two sporting internationals who have been members of ICC's staff. The earlier of these was Alec Morton, who joined the company as assistant accountant in 1934 and was subsequently promoted to be what would now be described as financial controller. Alec played soccer with Bohemians Football Club and had been selected for the first time in the late 1920s to play for Ireland's amateur team. So dedicated was he to the cause of amateur football that, having been a life-long committee member of Bohemians Football Club, he resigned from that club when it became professional. Morton was much in demand in soccer's administrative circles because of his accountancy skills and his knowledge of procedure at company and committee meetings. His international status ensured that he was also an unusually well-travelled man for those days, and he was guaranteed a spell-bound audience in his favourite hostelry when he talked about some of his foreign experiences. He was a good raconteur who was prepared to sacrifice strict accuracy in the interests of achieving dramatic effect. One can imagine him, like Seán O'Casey's Captain Boyle, seeking to impress his listeners by declaiming: 'I seen things that no mortal man should speak about that knows his Catechism'.

The other sporting international on the ICC staff was Donal Lenihan who, for a while in the 1980s, worked in ICC's Cork office. Donal was, of course, not only a rugby international, but also captain of the Irish rugby team and subsequently president of the Irish Rugby Football Union. He also went on to complete a term as manager of the Irish international team, and has recently been appointed as manager of the forthcoming Lions tour of Australia in 2001.

To end this chapter in light-hearted vein, there was the proposal which unusually proved not to be a proposal. A man, who did not look like a businessman, called to ICC's Limerick office and treated the receptionist to a lengthy and somewhat agitated discourse. His words were almost incomprehensible but the word 'bitch' occurred with such frequency that the receptionist thought that she was being verbally abused. Eventually the truth dawned on both her and the visitor. He had come to ICC in the mistaken belief that it housed the offices of the Irish Coursing Club, and he had been discussing the merits of a female greyhound, not the demerits of the receptionist.

18

Each Venture is a New Beginning

The world of venture capital (or, as it is often known now, private equity) is very different from the world of banking. A bank is concerned primarily with security and repayment prospects, while a venture capital proposition depends primarily on profit growth potential. This does not mean that the banker is mean-spirited by nature and that, on the other hand, the venture capitalist has a happy-go-lucky approach. Banking depends on such narrow margins that risks have to be carefully measured. Venture capital investment involves risks, and heavy losses when a business fails or turns in a lack-lustre performance. On the other hand, handsome profits can be made when the equity in an investee company increases significantly in value.

Since its inception ICC has always had a special affection for equity. In its early days this manifested itself mainly in raising capital through the stock exchange; as ICC was the main underwriter, there was the possibility, often the likelihood, that some of the shares would fall into its lap. Sometimes ICC subscribed initially for all the shares which were to be floated on the stock exchange and then, when the time was judged to be right, the shares so acquired were the subject of an offer for sale to the public. There were also occasions, admittedly few in the early days, when ICC subscribed directly for shares, with no specific take-out programme in mind. In one such case, the share subscription was made because the company concerned was in dire financial straits and would have collapsed but for the injection of funds brought about by ICC's share subscription. That subscription was made in the late 1930s. It did not prove possible to sell the shares to the public until ten years later. Happily, the company completely overcame these early difficulties and is still a prosperous enterprise.

One of ICC's difficulties in undertaking share subscriptions has been its lack of interest-free funds. To subscribe for shares, which in the short run will pay little or no dividend, is difficult when the ICC subscription has to be financed with interest-bearing monies received from depositors. Admittedly a good investment should more than pay its way in the long run but, in the meantime, the mismatch of funds can lead to short-term losses. If this were done on a large scale, it could have serious implications for a financial institution. However, this disincentive to invest heavily did not deter ICC totally from making share subscriptions. In most cases, the shares which ICC purchased yielded a rich harvest in due course. Very often the share investment was made because the company which required funds did not have the borrowing capacity to supply all its financial needs with a straightforward loan.

It should not be inferred from the foregoing that ICC had the luxury of being able to pick and choose its equity involvements from a queue of companies seeking finance in that form. Only in recent years have attitudes changed. Until the late 1980s there was a marked reluctance, especially in family businesses, to let outsiders participate in the equity – 'what we have, we hold' seems to have been their watchword. The entrepreneurs of those days very often failed to realise that to own 80 per cent of a thriving organisation could be much more satisfying and remunerative than to have total ownership of a pedestrian business. These attitudes were, in part, conditioned in earlier years by the predatory nature of some of the providers of risk capital, who sought big share-holdings and huge returns in return for relatively modest subscriptions. Unfortunately the activities of some of these operators led to adverse reaction to the venture capital industry; such reaction naturally affected concerns like ICC which, while seeking to benefit from its investments, wished to be fair to its customers.

A recurring theme in ICC's annual reports has been its venture capital activity. By 1987 ICC's total business had reached a stage of profitability where it was possible to market its venture capital wares more aggressively. Furthermore, it was evident that there was a growing interest in seeking venture capital, and businesspeople were beginning to be more receptive to the idea of admitting outside shareholders. It was decided, therefore, to establish ICC Venture Capital as a separate division. The build-up of the new division's portfolio started slowly and gained momentum from the early 1990s.

Associated with an enormous change in the business environment in Ireland, there has been an increasing interest by Irish business executives in having a shareholding in companies in which they work. Traditionally Irish executives have been employees rather than owners/entrepreneurs. The way to own one's business was to be the founder of it. A new option which emerged was to buy the business in which one worked – the Management Buy-Out (MBO). Opportunities to do so arose in a variety of circumstances. For example, some companies decided to concentrate on their core activities and their subsidiaries became available for acquisition; other family-owned companies were sold off because of a lack of succession or simply a desire on the part of the owners to realise the fruits of their labours. While MBOs are the most usual way of effecting sales of this kind, there is also the Management Buy-In (MBI), where the purchasers are managers from other businesses.

ICC Venture Capital has been active in investing in these opportunities and the experience has been very satisfactory. The presence of ICC Venture Capital as a shareholder is seen by prospective customers, suppliers and employees as positive and, apart from enhancing the capital base of the business, is an endorsement of its quality and growth ambitions. A measure of the success of ICC Venture Capital is that since 1987 its investments have generated a gross internal rate of return of nearly 22 per cent per annum. This compares very favourably with the Irish Stock Exchange Index (ISEQ) of just over 11 per cent per annum in the same period. At the end of 1999 unrealised gains from ICC's investment portfolio were almost £30 million.

A major development took place in 1994 when the ICC Venture Capital Fund was launched with external participation. Before this, all investments by ICC Venture Capital were funded directly by ICC itself. During 1993 and 1994 discussions took place between the government and the Irish Association of Pension Funds and the Irish Association of Investment Managers, with a view to making available some funds under management for investment in growing private Irish companies. It was agreed that some £50 million would be earmarked for venture capital investment through specialist venture capital fund managers. Accordingly, ICC launched its first venture capital fund of £20 million. The 1994 fund was fully invested and has been very successful. This new development in Ireland was in line with the international practice of adding private equity to the more traditional investments (quoted shares, property and fixed interest securities) made by fund managers. However, Ireland still has a long way to go compared with the United States where it is estimated that, on average, 7 per cent of pension fund assets are allocated to private equity, or even with the United Kingdom where the corresponding average is 0.9 per cent; the Irish figure is less than 0.4 per cent.

In April 1999, following the success of the 1994 fund, all the investors in that fund, together with some other institutions and a number of international investors, including the European Investment Bank and a large Dutch venture capital company, participated in a new £100 million fund known as ICC Private Equity Fund. This has made ICC the largest Irish provider of venture capital and it is the only bank which includes venture capital as part of its core business.

ICC can be justifiably proud of its pioneering role as the first Irish institution to recognise the software sector's potential by providing it with venture capital. ICC Venture Capital, in association with Enterprise Ireland, manages and has invested in the ICC Software Fund of £10 million. The sector is one of the outstanding success stories of Irish business, consisting as it does of some 750 companies employing more than 23,000 people. ICC also invested 25 per cent of the 1994 fund in software/information technology and this percentage will be even higher in the Private Equity Fund.

In May 2000 ICC Venture Capital launched the new £100 million ICC Software 2000 Fund. This fund aims to capitalise on the booming growth of the software sector by investing in companies with software technologies or business applications specifically for niche markets.

Not everything in the venture capital world has been plain sailing. In its earlier days the main shareholders in a business would sometimes offer to buy back the shares which ICC held. Even if such a request seemed reasonable, it was not always received with open arms. It was hard to resist the suspicion that ICC was not hearing the entire story. Perhaps there was a take-over bid in the wind or a dramatic improvement in profits. If either possibility was real, ICC had no desire to make an early exit.

The workload of the venture capitalist is considerable. In order to make one investment, many potential investee companies have to be examined and assessed to see if the management team are capable, ambitious and trustworthy. (Within ICC, these qualities are summarised in the acronym CAT, the feline sound of which suggests an appropriate opportunism.) The making of the investment is also a complex and time-consuming matter. Once the investment is made, an ICC nominee is usually appointed to the board of the investee company. The progress of the business is monitored and efforts are made to enhance its worth by growth.

Occasionally there is some light relief, as instanced by the following tale. Few of ICC's customers wore their religion on their sleeves, but the proprietor of one investee company was pleased to do so. One year he made his annual visit to Lourdes and came home via Paris. On his return to Ireland, he said that he had enjoyed a visit to the Folies Bergères. When surprise was expressed at this apparent deviation from his normal high moral standards, he replied that he had gone there because, for all its worldliness, the show contained the most beautiful dramatisation of the Ave Maria that he had ever had the pleasure to experience.

But this is a long way from the serious business of making equity investments. A recent examination of the make-up of ICC's investments shows that half of them are used for expansion, 22 per cent for MBOs and MBIs, 16 per cent for re-structuring businesses, and the balance for start-up ventures. If there is any area of venture capital where there can be a shortage of available funds, it is in the start-up area. The risks in brand-new ventures are naturally much higher than in established businesses, as it is almost impossible to predict sales and costs with any certainty. It would, therefore, be unreasonable to expect a high proportion of a venture capitalist's portfolio to be devoted to neophytes. When the National Development Corporation (Nadcorp) was established by the state in the 1980s, it set out to fill this gap and did so for a time. Then a government decision was taken to wind up Nadcorp. This left a major vacuum; start-up and seed capital are still difficult to raise.

Even though in absolute terms venture capital is a small proportion of the total finance invested by ICC, it is, nevertheless, a very profitable and growing area and one in which ICC has carved out an important niche for itself. Through its own investments and those procured from fund managers, it has made a significant amount of risk capital available to growing Irish companies. It is certain that the founding fathers, with their affection for equity, would have approved generally of what has been done by ICC in this area. One cannot help feeling, however, that, in the more conservative era in which they lived, they might have raised an eyebrow at the tendency for professional managers to become involved in serious share acquisition rather than remaining content with their salaried lot.

19
Ireland's Business Bank

T he 1990s were economically the most successful decade in the history of the state. Not that the early years of the decade gave too much cause for optimism. In 1990 there were economic uncertainties throughout the world and, although the Irish economy was beginning to improve, the wounds of the late 1980s were not yet healed. Even the anticipated recovery seemed at first to be a false dawn. There had been expectations that the United Kingdom and the United States would emerge from recession quickly, but this did not happen and so domestic economic activity slowed down, not helped by interest rates reverting to particularly high levels.

The most worrying crisis in interest rates occurred in the autumn and winter of 1992 on foot of threatened currency devaluations. Business failures began to increase. This was not surprising at a time when retail interest rates averaged 35 per cent and sometimes exceeded 40 per cent. In the whole-sale market, the situation was even worse, with overnight rates occasionally approaching 100 per cent. The difficulties for business were enormous. Not alone were interest rates unbelievably high but, until the Irish pound was re-aligned in the European Monetary System early in 1993 and consequently was realigned against sterling, business suffered from extreme fluctuations in costs. To help its customers to overcome these problems, ICC sometimes provided loans on terms which yielded minimal profit.

The report of the Industrial Policy Review Group, *A Time for Change: Industrial Policy for the 1990s* (the Culliton Report), was published at the beginning of 1992, and made many important recommendations, especially in the area of grants, taxation, infrastructure and education. It is of interest that, although the economy was in the doldrums at the time the report was published, the chairman, Jim Culliton, in his preface, struck what proved to be the right note when he wrote: 'The next decade will provide greater opportunities for enterprise and initiative than we have ever seen before. The extent to which our community will accept this challenge will determine our future levels of employment and national wealth' (Department of Industry and Commerce, 1992: p.7).

The Irish economic boom did not commence until 1994 but it has continued apace since then. Lower interest rates and high budget surpluses have become the order of the day. Ireland's economic growth is now the highest in the European Union and indeed in the OECD. Exports are substantially higher, corporate profits have risen, and employment has increased significantly – from 1,110,000 in 1989 to 1,543,000 in 1999. During its lifetime ICC has seen and contributed substantially to a four-fold growth in manufacturing employment.

Needless to say, the Ireland of the 'eurozone' is not entirely a paradise. There is still a good deal of poverty, despite some improvements in social services. There are other aspects of the social scene which are disturbing, notably homelessness and the heavy incidence of drug-taking. The house property boom has caused major problems for would-be purchasers, particularly for young people seeking to acquire their first house. While the setting up of state tribunals is nothing new for Ireland, it is an unwelcome development that the establishment of so many tribunals was found necessary during the 1990s. However, notwithstanding these negative features, Ireland at the beginning of the twenty-first century is stronger economically than at any time in the history of the state.

On the political front, the 1990s were unique in that, throughout the period, there was a succession of coalition governments. In the past there have been coalitions but generally they were both preceded and succeeded by one-party regimes. In the 1990s there were four different coalition governments. No longer is the concept of coalition deemed to be unacceptable and, indeed, government by coalition seems likely to continue for the foreseeable future.

This brief overview of the economic, social and political scene in the 1990s sets the background against which the most dramatic change in ICC has taken place since its establishment. During the late 1980s ICC, as we have seen, had been shedding its developmental role. It was abundantly clear that the Ireland of the late twentieth century had a comprehensive banking service and that the need for the state to play a developmental role in industrial and commercial finance had virtually disappeared. The various ministerial and other observations emanating from the Department of Finance showed that the department would not be averse to a disposal of ICC to commercial interests, if the price was considered satisfactory. Thus began the task of converting what had been one of the strongest development banks in the world into a specialist business bank, which would continue to fill a niche in the market and generate a commercial rate of return for its owners.

The government first publicly demonstrated its appetite for a change in the ownership of ICC in 1990. The then Minister for Finance, Albert Reynolds, appointed Stokes Kennedy Crowley (now KPMG) to advise him on the future developments and capital requirements of ICC. That ICC was already prepared for the major change which lay ahead is shown by the chairman's statement at the annual general meeting of 1991. He said:

> The broadening of ICC's services and the re-orientation of the company as a competitive force specialising in the finan-cial needs of business have been possible because of the commitment and hard work of the management and staff, as well as the support of my co-directors and the directors of our subsidiary companies. The result of these combined efforts is reflected in the strong level of business and the record profits achieved in the past year.

The year 1991 was a milestone in the history of ICC: Michael

Quinn became its fourth managing director in December of that year. Michael had joined ICC in 1972 and, since then, had been a spectacular performer, firstly as an executive, and subsequently as a member of general management. The appointment of Michael Quinn was widely welcomed both inside and outside ICC. To him would fall the onerous task of leading ICC towards its new status as an outstanding specialist business bank.

Soon after Michael Quinn's appointment as managing director, Jim Barton's period of office as chairman came to an end and he was succeeded by E. A. (Ted) MacRedmond, a leading and much admired figure in the insurance industry. Ted MacRedmond had a considerable knowledge of the Irish business scene. His friends and associates speak of his great loyalty. Like his predecessor, Ted was a racing enthusiast and the high point of his year was the annual Tralee race meeting. He was a keen golfer and was renowned for his prodigious tee-shots. He arrived at ICC in a year when the business environment was still difficult. Nevertheless, the company's profit showed a 20 per cent increase in that year.

ICC's rapid progression towards change was marked by the passing of the ICC Bank Act of 1992. Apart from further increasing the company's borrowing powers to £1.3 billion, the Act allowed ICC to intensify its strategy of specialisation in the corporate banking market across a broader cross-section of business and without any geographic restrictions. The Act also provided for a change in the name of the company to ICC Bank plc and brought it under the super-vision of the Central Bank. The change of name would certainly have appealed to the members of the first ICC board, who had frequently voiced their displeasure at the original name, The Industrial Credit Company, Limited. They thought it gave the false impression that they were engaged in one of the less reputable areas of banking. The 1992 change of name was not, of course, cosmetic but was designed to emphasise the essential difference between ICC as it had been and the business bank it was becoming. In 1993 ICC duly celebrated this transitional move with a record pre-tax profit.

Patrick Twohig V. G. Supermarket, Kanturk, County Cork - one of ICC's first customers for distribution finance in the late 1960s.

The final inspection department of Semperit (Ireland) Limited, Ballyfermot, Dublin, a customer of ICC, which was a significant employer from the time of its establishment in the late 1960s.

One of the pieces of equipment produced by Crown Controls Limited, Galway – an ICC customer in the early 1970s.

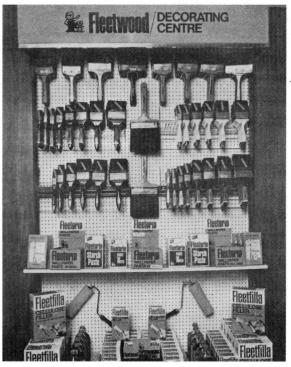

A display of some products from Fleetwoood Limited, Dublin, a family partnership, which was a customer of ICC's in the early 1970s.

At a Board meeting in ICC's Merrion Square offices, in 1971.
L to R: Samuel F. Thompson, Dr. C. K. Mill, J. J. O'Leary, James P.
Beddy (Chairman), Frank Casey (the author), M. W. O'Reilly,
Joseph Griffin.

ICC's first Limerick
office, opened 1974.

Albert Reynolds, TD (centre), as Minister for Transport, was the chief guest at the first showing of the film Mayo – A County on the Move *in 1981. The film was partly funded by ICC.*

The then Minister for Industry, Commerce & Tourism, Desmond O'Malley, TD (third from left), with winners of the Mid-West Craft Awards in 1982, organised jointly by ICC and Shannon Development.

At the ICC Golden Jubilee Lecture in 1983 were L-R: Frank Casey (the author), Alan Dukes, TD, then Minister for Finance, and the speaker, Professor Dermot McAleese, TCD.

A meeting of the European Club of Long Term Financing Institutions hosted by ICC Bank at Dublin Castle in 1983.

Michael Mortell discussing further plans for his fashion business with Charles Carroll of ICC in the early 1980s.

A visit of EIB Senior Management to Birex pharmaceutical company, Stillorgan Industrial Estate, County Dublin in 1984.

In 1986 the then Minister for Finance, John Bruton TD (centre), increased the Bank's issued share capital as ICC moved towards an increasingly commercial role. Pictured with the Minister were, from left, Jim Barton (Chairman) and Frank Casey (the author).

Kennedy practising before his performance at the National Concert Hall, Dublin in 1990 sponsored by ICC.

Michael Aherne (ICC), Eugene Murtagh (Chairman, Kingspan) and Richard Dennis (President, Irish Stock Exchange) at the flotation of Kingspan on the Irish Stock Exchange in 1989.

An Taoiseach, Bertie Ahern, TD (left), then Minister for Finance, at the opening of ICC's new Dealing Room in 1992 with the late Brendan Murphy (centre) and Dermot Dolan of ICC.

ICC's office in Eyre Square Shopping Centre, Galway. The bank opened its first office in Galway in 1992.

Madison Hotel, Belfast, part of the bank's wide ranging portfolio in Northern Ireland which has been growing steadily since ICC opened its Belfast office in 1996.

Ruairi Quinn, TD, when Minister for Finance in 1997, introduced legislation which provided for a substantial increase in ICC Bank's authorised share capital and borrowing powers to allow for continued expansion of the Bank's activities.

Stuart Parker (left) and Henk Groenen (right) of NMB-Heller with Michael Quinn of ICC Bank at the signing of a new joint venture partnership, ICC-Heller, in 1998 to provide confidential invoice discounting for business.

Datalex Travel Solutions, one of ICC's expanding software venture capital investments.

Representatives of the participating banks at the signing of ICC's largest syndicated loan to date, for €900 million, at Tulfarris House, September 1999.

Some members of the Cork staff outside ICC House, Cork. ICC has had a presence in Cork since 1969.

International participants at a recent ICC Consulting seminar, part of the Bank's growing international training and consultancy activities.

ICC's Property Division participated in syndicated funding for the development of the successful Jervis Shopping Centre in Dublin.

Charlie McCreevy, TD, Minister for Finance, (seated left), with Phil Flynn, Chairman (seated right), and Michael Quinn, Managing Director, discussing ICC Bank's proposals for the new millennium.

While ICC was increasingly a commercial bank, it found time in 1994 to make a submission to the government-appointed Small Business Task Force. In the light of that submission, the government appointed the company to manage its Small Business Expansion Loan Scheme (SBEL). This scheme was created to provide much-needed fixed-rate finance for small and medium-sized businesses, following a year of major fluctuations in interest rates. ICC raised £100 million for on-lending at an attractive rate which included a state subsidy. The SBEL was availed of by almost 500 firms and guaranteed nearly 4,000 jobs. Despite ICC's move away from development banking, it was still recognised as an organisation that could efficiently discharge a specific business-focused scheme that required management and specialised expertise.

Generally, 1994 was a highly successful year for ICC. Profit again reached record levels. The Galway office, which had functioned as a treasury representative office since it was established in 1992, soon moved to the larger premises which it now occupies in Eyre Square Shopping Centre. Here it enjoys the status of a full branch office. A new treasury representative office was opened in Waterford.

However, the company also suffered a great loss when one of its general managers, Brendan Murphy, died at an early age. Brendan had joined ICC as a bright young graduate from University College, Cork, in 1969, when ICC's first Cork office was opened. He brought with him a fresh approach and an enthusiasm which remained with him throughout his career in ICC, during which he was frequently promoted, becoming a general manager in 1987. In his spare time Brendan was a first-rate athlete. On several occasions he finished in the first twenty in the Dublin City Marathon. Because of his great fitness, his early death was a particularly great shock to everyone, not least to the chief executive, Michael Quinn, whose brother-in-law he was. As Brendan's wife, Anne, had been my personal assistant for several years, my own sense of loss was intensified by the deep sympathy I felt for her and her young family. Several other colleagues – Des Byrne, Tom Dawson, Betty Doyle, Michael Maher,

Michael Rodgers, Noirin McSharry and Pat Tracey – have
died in office over the years. Their part in the many ICC
successes mentioned in these pages was considerable. They
and others, like former company secretary Tom Donnelly, are
remembered with affection and respect by all who worked
with them.

In 1995, another year of record profit, the treasury
subsidiary, ICC Investment Bank, which had been established
in 1993, was able to announce that it had reached a total of
£300 million for deposits, this in addition to the government
guaranteed deposits (£1 billion at their peak) raised by the
parent company. A decision was taken to open a full branch
in Belfast; this would happen in the following year but, in the
meantime, ICC made its first investment in a project wholly
based in Northern Ireland. Because of the legislation of 1992,
ICC had no legal difficulty in making this investment, but the
first directors would certainly have recalled their disappointment during the 1930s when they sought a legal opinion,
which proved to be negative, on the feasibility of financing
even cross-Border projects.

In March 1996 Phil Flynn was appointed chairman in
succession to Ted MacRedmond, to become the seventh
chairman in the company's history. Phil Flynn is a former
general secretary of the trade union IMPACT, a former
president of the Irish Congress of Trade Unions, a director
of the Voluntary Health Insurance Board and a well-known
mediator and negotiator in difficult industrial disputes. I
first met Phil Flynn when we served together on the board
of the Institute of Public Administration. His contributions
to the Institute were always well considered and valuable,
and I know that they were always appreciated by his colleagues on the board and, in particular, by the
director-general of the Institute, John Gallagher. ICC is very
fortunate to have as its current chairman someone with his
exceptional qualities.

The company operated in a strong economic environment
in 1996, although it had to face intense competition. A
particularly successful area was tourism, where ICC estimated
that it had reached 25 per cent of its target market. ICC

Investment Bank was again able to announce a major success – the raising of a £115-million facility from a syndicate of international banks. This facility was raised without a state guarantee and illustrated the growing independence and financial standing of ICC.

In 1997, despite contracting lending margins arising from lower interest rates, the company turned in another record profit. It was handsomely exceeded in the two subsequent years, when profit grew by about 20 per cent in each year. This does not include the substantial unrealised gains on ICC's venture capital investments. The net profit, before exceptional items, for the year ended 31 October 1999 was £25.2 million. ICC, which had struggled to pay a maiden dividend of 2.5 per cent in 1940, was able just under sixty years later to declare a well-covered dividend amounting to £4.5 million. In the ten years to October 1999, ICC's dividends, together with the tax charge, amounted to more than £60 million, a worthwhile contribution to exchequer funds.

The share capital was significantly augmented by a rights issue for £15 million in September 1998. In the same year ICC Investment Bank raised another revolving credit facility. This time, the amount was expressed in euros (€350 million). There was again no state guarantee and the facility was the first-ever euro-syndicated loan raised by an Irish borrower. It was not a great year internationally as the Asian economic crisis affected economic growth. However, the Irish economy continued to boom and, as has been shown, so have ICC's trading results. In September 1999 ICC raised yet another record euroloan of €900 million, the largest Irish syndicated loan up to that time. ICC's international standing was further enhanced with the significant over-subscription to its first transaction of the twenty-first century, despite some international concerns at the excessive rate of growth of the Irish economy. The €500 million facility signed in June 2000 means that ICC funding from syndicated loans since 1997 has been almost £2 billion. The growth of ICC's business during the 1990s is reflected in the fact that its assets, which were slightly more than £1 billion in 1990, increased to almost £2.5

billion by the end of the financial period to 31 October 1999.

Furthermore, the healthy profit growth has continued into the present century. In the six months to April 2000 the net profit was £18.3 million, a 64 per cent increase on the corresponding figure for the previous year.

At the beginning of the twenty-first century ICC is a strong, specialised business bank. It has behind it a record of achievement. Encouraged by past success, it has, in the words of Michael Quinn, set itself 'challenging targets' and it is poised to continue its progress as another chapter in its history begins.

20

ICC – An Arch to Build Upon

It is difficult to describe Ireland's progress as a nation concisely, but the Welsh writer Jan Morris has produced a succinct sentence: 'Nowhere in western Europe has history moved faster than in Ireland – which in this century has matured from a hang-dog, rebellious and poverty-stricken British possession to a confident and progressive sovereign member of the European Community' (1998: p. 132).

The young state began life shortly after World War 1 when trading was difficult. It then suffered from the effects of a civil war and, later on, the economic depression which followed the Wall Street crisis of 1929. In the 1930s a new government introduced a protectionist policy, but also engaged in an economic war with Ireland's principal customer, Great Britain. Then World War 2 broke out and, while Ireland remained neutral and avoided the worst effects of this universal conflict, its economic progress was retarded. It was not until the first *Programme for Economic Expansion* was launched in 1958 that major development occurred. There followed the buoyant 1960s, the less happy 1970s with a succession of oil crises, and the inflationary and debt-ridden 1980s. Even the 1990s did not begin too well but, since 1994, there has been an unprecedented improvement in the economy, with much lower levels of unemployment, a noticeable increase in the number and quality of Irish entrepreneurs, significant budget surpluses and a general atmosphere of well-being.

ICC, although it is a relatively small financial institution, can reasonably claim to have played an important and innovative part in the country's economic development. The public flotations of the 1930s were a brave pioneering effort by the first board and management. But they were much more than that. In its first forty years ICC sponsored more than half the public flotations in the Irish market. It played a key role in building up interest in the Irish Stock Exchange and, indeed, contributed in no small measure to the substantial increase in the number of companies quoted on that exchange. Without such activity, it would not have been possible to finance the establishment of many new industries. These industries provided much-needed employment and training for workers, who would otherwise have had difficulty in earning a living in the depressed Ireland of the years before and after World War 2. Furthermore, it is certain that the intense activity in the Irish Stock Exchange of today has been greatly helped by being built on a strong foundation, to which ICC contributed so much.

But ICC did not rest on its laurels. When the state became more active in encouraging industrial development, ICC played its part in directly financing the new ventures thereby established. Having started as an issuing house, which engaged in a limited amount of lending activity, it developed an increasingly wide range of services to meet the growing needs of its customers. Having confined itself almost entirely to industry in its early days, it broadened its field of endeavour to meet the demands of important areas of business like the distributive sector, property development and the tourist industry. In so doing, it made a worthwhile contribution to the substantial growth in employment which has occurred, particularly in the 1990s.

After a somewhat unpropitious start, ICC enjoyed a good relationship with its sponsoring department, the Department of Finance. ICC's innovations have generally been encouraged and have often been welcomed to such an extent that practical support was forthcoming. ICC's dealings with the World Bank and the European Investment Bank were aided substantially by the positive support that was forthcoming from the department. The company was also assisted by the willingness of the government to bring forward amending legislation when it was deemed necessary. The ICC Bank Act of 1992, which stripped away virtually all limitations on ICC's lending activities, the ICC Bank (Amendment) Act of 1997 and the ICC Bank Act of 1999, which allowed for increases in the bank's share capital and borrowing powers, were the most recent in a long line of legislative changes designed to help ICC to meet new demands and challenges.

Over the years ICC has had many successes and occasional failures. Any attempt to itemise the successes would be misguided, as such a list would almost certainly exclude some companies that should have been included. The company with which ICC is probably proudest to have been associated is Roadstone Limited, which ICC supported from its earliest days until it became a major part of CRH plc, one of Ireland's largest and most successful industries. ICC also supported from its inception Cement Limited, the other main constituent of CRH plc.

Not all ICC's loans and investments were successful. Earlier in this book there is an account of the efforts made to save Cloth Manufacturers Limited, Cootehill. That is but one example of the extent to which ICC was prepared to go if there was some prospect of rescuing a troubled business. Nor had all the innovations a satisfactory outcome. ICC could have enjoyed a near-perfect record if it had shown a smaller appetite for risks. But if it had done this, it would not have been an effective development bank and it might not have become the successful business bank that it is today.

There must be a danger that one who was very close to ICC for most of his working life may view it through rose-coloured spectacles. I hope that this is not the case. I believe that ICC played a significant part in the state's economic development. ICC was established to fill a gap in the Irish financial world and it filled that gap competently and successfully. Throughout its existence ICC, although it has always been profitable, has been particularly conscious of the needs of small and medium-sized businesses and, as a business bank, it continues to direct its main attention to those enterprises.

Since its establishment, it has been involved in venture capital and has considerably increased its activities in that area in recent years. Whatever it has embarked upon, be it underwriting, lending, asset financing, investing or consulting, it has given of its best. A recent unpublished academic study of ethics in Irish banking has found that ICC is one of two banks whose ethical standards are outstandingly higher than those of all the other banks.

James Cawley, a well-known solicitor, who was a member of the ICC board during the 1980s, has summarised his impressions and experiences as a director:

> Although I had plenty of experience of the commercial scene, my appointment to the ICC board was my first opportunity to see the inside workings of a banking institution. I was impressed by the quality and professionalism of the management and the care with which proposals were prepared. One was always conscious of the desire of management to look after the interests of the customers as well as those of ICC. There was an excellent working relationship between board and management which made it a real pleasure to attend board meetings.

This book has attempted to describe ICC and some of those who guided its fortunes over the years. It has also sought to place the activities of ICC during various periods since its incorporation in the context of the economic and social conditions of those periods. While it has dealt with the many worthwhile aspects of ICC's development, it has not set out to suggest that all is or has been perfect in ICC's world. I have been associated with ICC through many of its triumphs and occasional vicissitudes. I have worked with and met many excellent people whose primary concern was the national interest rather than any personal self-advancement. ICC was a respected development bank and, today, it is a business bank that has not forgotten that it exists to help business and not simply to make a profit for its shareholders. Based on past history, there can be little doubt that it will continue to serve both business and its shareholders well.

Appendix 1
What is a Development Bank?

ICC is referred to frequently in this book as a development bank. A precise definition of a development bank is not as easy as it seems, especially since many of the early development banks, including ICC, did not originally describe themselves as such. The term only came into general usage with the establishment of such banks in many developing countries in the post-war years with the assistance of the World Bank. These were usually described as DFIs – development finance institutions. In Europe, several banks of this kind were set up in response to the needs of their countries' devastated economies after World War 2. With the passing of the years and the improvement of those economies, most of these banks have become increasingly commercial.

DFIs come in all shapes and sizes. Some are owned wholly or in part by the state, while others are privately owned. They may have a profit motive, especially if they fall into the latter category, or they may be lenders of last resort, required to do nothing more than pay their way. The range of their activities is also varied. Some are set up to help industry only. Others, the great majority, cover a wide range of businesses. There are DFIs which finance only the private sector, while others are used by the state as channels for the investment of monies in state-owned enterprises. Some DFIs even offer incentives such as grants.

Probably the first DFI in the world was the Industrial Bank of Japan, which was established just before the end of the nineteenth century. Between then and World War 1, such banks were set up in a few other countries. Ireland was not the first European country to have a DFI, but it was among the earliest.

Most countries now have a long-term credit institution, which at some stage in its history could have been described as a DFI. In the European Union practically every country has such an institution and representatives of these banks, including ICC, meet at regular intervals to share their experiences and report on any new initiatives they may have taken. Rather than describe all these banks, it is more instructive to compare ICC with two other long-term institutions both of which, although very different from each other in their establishment and operation, had some similarities to ICC. The two banks are the Industrial Development Bank (IDB) of Canada, and the Industrial and Commercial Finance Corporation (ICFC) in the United Kingdom.

IDB was established in 1944 by a Canadian act of parliament. The first directors of ICC had made it clear that they disliked the name 'The Industrial Credit Company'. It is of interest, therefore, that in Canada there was also much debate about the title of their new development bank. Those who devised the legislation used the name 'Industrial Credit Bank' in early drafts, and it was not until much later that the word 'development' was substituted for 'credit'. The rationale for the change was that 'credit' suggested a kind of short-term accommodation, usually provided by the commercial banks. While IDB was a state-owned institution, its shares were held, not by the state directly, but by the Bank of Canada, which is owned by the state. IDB was conceived as a lender of last resort, which would only offer financial assistance if its board was of the opinion that funds would not otherwise be available to the applicant on reasonable terms.

In its early days IDB was very much restricted to industry, but later legislation enabled it to deal with most sectors. It was not encouraged to take up equity, and when it did it was required to do so only with a view to re-sale. The legislation setting up the bank was in one respect more explicit than ICC's legislation because IDB was required to give particular consideration to the problems of small enterprises. As IDB was supposed to be a lender of last resort, it often ran into problems with the commercial banks in Canada, as it believed that some of these banks tended to wait until IDB had assessed a proposition and would then try to take the business for themselves. Eventually, in the 1970s, IDB was absorbed into the Federal Business Development Bank (FBDB), a larger organisation with wider powers and, unlike IDB, the opportunity to make the taking of equity stakes a major part of the business.

The British experience was very different. As far back as 1929 the Treasury had set up a commission on finance and industry, under the chairmanship of H. R. MacMillan, a Scottish lawyer who became a lord in 1930. The commission reported in 1931 that there was a gap in the supply of medium and long-term capital up to £200,000 for small businesses. This gap became known as the 'MacMillan gap'. The gap still exists. According to an article in the May 1999 issue of *Director*, a survey by the British Federation of Small Businesses has shown that 65 per cent of small and medium-sized businesses in the UK do not have term loans but rely on overdraft facilities.

Presumably because of the Great Depression and World War 2, action on the MacMillan report was delayed but, eventually, in 1945, the British government announced that the English and Scottish banks would be setting up two new financial institutions – the Industrial and Commercial Finance Corporation (ICFC) to provide finance for smaller business, and Finance Corporation for Industry (FCI) to help large companies. There was initially no government holding in either of these companies. The Bank of England, which was then privately owned, held 3 per cent of the equity of ICFC and 15 per cent of FCI. Subsequently these holdings came under state ownership, when the Bank of England was nationalised. Ultimately the two companies were welded together into a larger company, Investors in Industry, which, in due course, was given the name 3i. That company later went public and could not now by any stretch of the imagination be described as a DFI.

One of ICFC's superficial similarities to ICC was that both, in their early days, had very inadequate accommodation. Indeed, it appears that ICC's initial accommodation, poor though it was, was palatial compared to the two rooms which ICFC occupied on the attic floor of the office of the London branch of a New Zealand bank. From commencement, ICFC was always interested in equity. As far as possible, when it made a loan it also acquired a small equity stake in the borrowing company. Some of these equity stakes were, in due course, to lead to enormous profits for ICFC. One, which is often mentioned, is British Caledonian Airways, the shares of which had languished on the books of ICFC for years but suddenly became very valuable when British Airways took over British Caledonian. ICFC was not restricted in the kind of business it could handle. However, it had problems with its shareholders, the commercial banks, some of whom were very sensitive to ICFC taking on business that the banks might have been happy to finance. As the years went by, the nature of ICFC changed. It began as a lending organisation which took equity stakes, but, by the time it was absorbed into 3i, it was a venture capital company which provided loans where these were needed to complete a financial package.

The foregoing shows that ICC, as a DFI, fitted somewhere between the two extremes represented by IDB and ICFC. Like IDB, ICC was effectively owned by the state and had to accept some initial restrictions on the sectors it could finance, although not as many as the Canadian company. Like ICFC, it started life as a lender which took equity stakes but, although its underwriting activities were relatively larger than those of ICFC, its venture capital portfolio was developed much more slowly. Both IDB and ICFC had, for different reasons, difficulties with the commercial banks. In its early days, ICC had no such difficulties and, even when it has been in open competition with the Irish banks, relations between ICC and the banks have always been good. IDB was a lender of last resort and while ICFC did not wittingly discharge this role, its sister organisation, FCI, was so designated and sustained very heavy losses in carrying out its mandate. ICC was not a lender of last resort but, conscious of its developmental role, adopted a more tolerant attitude towards companies in difficulties than might have been expected from a cold-bloodedly commercial organisation.

Appendix 2
Dr J. P. Beddy – An Appreciation
by Dr T. K. Whitaker

When the history of Irish industrial development comes to be written, the name of Dr J P Beddy will have the prominence and honour due to a pioneer. It was his quiet genius that brought from infancy to strength the financial and promotional institutions on which our industrial progress has been based.

For four decades, ever since he left the inspectorate of taxes in 1933 to join the newly-established Industrial Credit Company, as its first secretary, his gentle but authoritative hand has guided the evolution and expansion of Irish industry. He had become much more than secretary of the Industrial Credit Company before he succeeded the late J P Colbert as its managing director in 1952. Already he had equipped himself academically, as well as through experience, to perform a public service of the highest quality. The mature articulation of theory and practice which informed his analysis, assessment and organisational decisions was indicated even in the title of his thesis on 'Profits – Theoretical and Practical Aspects' published in 1940 and for which he received his Doctorate in Economic Science. He lectured for many years in UCD on economic geography.

When the Industrial Development Authority was established in 1950 as the official promotional agency he was the natural choice as its first chairman. He was also the first chairman of the grant-giving authority – An Foras Tionscal –

set up in 1952. He was then at the apex of the institutional system for both the promotion and the financing, through loans, share issues and grants, of Irish industry. He exercised his acuteness of judgement and gave his fair, well-considered and cogent advice on all the major projects of the fifties and sixties. He retired as chairman of the IDA in 1965, remained chairman and managing director of the ICC until 1969, staying on for a while afterwards as part-time chairman.

A shy man, he was yet the best of company, with a keen sense of humour, and discriminating taste. He preferred the excellent in moderation to the good in abundance – a single Corona a day, a thimbleful of the best brandy at night.

Born in Cobh in 1900, he was later in the same class at O'Connell Schools in Dublin as Sean Lemass. He lost his heart to Kerry when he was an inspector of taxes in Tralee. He made his name on the Kerry bogs as one of the sharpest of snipe shooters. He was interested in sailing, too, but fishing was his most abiding love. Some of my happiest days were shared with him on Lough Inagh, where he would fish a purist's wet fly despite his rival's greater success with the 'dap' and would meticulously prepare tomato soup for lunch in the fishing hut.

Jim Beddy lived for his work and his family and his wife's death a few years ago created a great void. An expression of sympathy with his daughters, son and their families must contain a special word for his granddaughter, Maeve, whose companionship and love were always, and particularly in the latter years, a great comfort to him. A public servant who achieved much for Ireland, yet shrank from any praise or recognition for it, has gone to his eternal reward.

(Whitaker, 1983)

Appendix 3
Directors of ICC

Name	Period(s) of Appointment
Mr J. P. Colbert	October 1933 to August 1952
Mr T. Caffrey	October 1933 to April 1949
Dr L. J. Kettle	October 1933 to September 1960
Mr J. F. Punch	October 1933 to March 1943
Mr J. J. O'Leary	October 1933 to July 1971
Mr M. W. O'Reilly	March 1943 to July 1971
Dr J. P. Beddy	June 1949 to May 1972
Mr J. Griffin	September 1952 to July 1964
Dr C. K. Mill	March 1959 to March 1974
Mr S. F. Thompson	March 1959 to February 1982
Mr P. McDonald	December 1963 to January 1974
Mr P. Hughes	October 1964 to February 1977
Mr D. Herlihy	July 1971 to November 1976
Mr J. A. O'Connor	July 1971 to March 1973
Mr W. O'Brien	January 1973 to January 1975
	February 1978 to February 1984
Mr F. A. Casey	January 1974 to November 1991
Mr W. Corrigan	January 1974 to October 1980
Mr J. T. Barton	January 1975 to March 1992
Mr F. Mulcahy	January 1975 to February 1978
Mr M. McShane	February 1977 to July 1977
Mr J. H. D. Ryan	February 1977 to March 1989
Mr P. Kelly	July 1977 to February 1978
Mr J. G. Hickey	February 1978 to February 1987
Mr J. Cawley	October 1980 to March 1983
Mr J. A. Kerrigan	April 1982 to March 1985
Mr L. O'Donnell	March 1983 to March 1998
Mr M. Neville	July 1983 to August 1985
Mr N. Holland	February 1984 to March 1990
Mr P. A. White	February 1984 to March 1996
Mr M. Honan	March 1985 to March 1989
Mr P. C. Molloy	September 1985 to March 1993

Mr V. Daly	February 1987 to March 1995
Ms C. O'Connor	March 1989*
Mr J. McPeake	March 1989 to March 1997
	March 1998*
Mr E. Freaney	March 1990*
Mr M. Quinn	November 1991*
Mr E. A. MacRedmond	March 1992 to March 1996
Mr T. Considine	March 1993 to January 1998
	December 1998 to May 2000
Mr P. Flynn	March 1996*
Ms A. Connolly	March 1996 to March 1997
Mr S. Kelly	March 1996 to March 1999
Mr F. Ryan	March 1997 to May 2000
Mr D. Doyle	February 1998 to December 1998
Mr D. Miller	December 1998*
Mr M. Flynn	March 1999 - July 2000
Mr D. McNally	May 2000*
Mr P. Mackay	May 2000*

denotes current director

Notes

Mr J. P. Colbert	Chairman and Managing Director during his entire period as a Director (October 1933 to April 1952)
Dr J. P. Beddy	Chairman and Managing Director from June 1952 to May 1969 and Chairman from then until May 1972
Mr D. Herlihy	Chairman from May 1972 to November 1976
Mr F. A. Casey	Managing Director from July 1979 to November 1991
Mr J. T. Barton	Chairman from January 1977 to February 1979 and from February 1984 to March 1992
Mr J. G. Hickey	Chairman from February 1979 to February 1984
Mr M. Quinn	Current Managing Director, appointed to that position in December 1991
Mr E. A. MacRedmond	Chairman from March 1992 to March 1996
Mr P. Flynn	Current Chairman, appointed in March 1996

Appendix 4

Summary of Selected Balance Sheets of ICC, 1934 – 1999

Summary of Selected Balance Sheets at Historical Values

	31-Oct-34 £000	31-Oct-43 £000	31-Oct-53 £000	31-Oct-63 £000	31-Oct-73 £000	31-Oct-83 £000	31-Oct-93 £000	31-Oct-99 £000
Assets								
Loans	453	188	444	7,849	23,701	348,362	814,792	2,145,754
Debt and other fixed term securities	–	–	–	–	–	–	–	–
Investments	136	659	2,173	4,673	3,620	41,895	21,102	268,015
Other Assets	86	116	670	3,865	1,946	86,148	255,356	17,379
Preliminary expenses	13	–	–	–	–	–	–	20,409
Total Assets	688	963	3,287	16,387	29,267	476,405	1,091,250	2,451,557
Liabilities and Capital								
Creditors	170	70	1,372	6,417	18,382	447,463	986,118	2,226,515
Reserve Fund	–	50	100	–	–	–	–	–
Subordinated Liabilities	–	–	–	–	–	–	42,418	87,559
Shareholders' Funds	518	843	1,815	9,970	10,885	28,942	62,714	137,483
	688	963	3,287	16,387	29,267	476,405	1,091,250	2,451,557

Summary of Selected Balance Sheets adjusted for inflation

	31-Oct-34 £000	31-Oct-43 £000	31-Oct-53 £000	31-Oct-63 £000	31-Oct-73 £000	31-Oct-83 £000	31-Oct-93 £000	31-Oct-99 £000
Assets								
Loans	19,835	4,396	7,648	103,128	160,157	555,819	919,680	2,145,754
Debt and other fixed term securities	–	–	–	–	–	–	–	–
Investments	5,955	15,409	37,429	61,398	24,462	66,844	23,818	268,015
Other Assets	3,766	2,712	11,540	50,782	13,150	137,451	288,228	17,379
Preliminary expenses	569	–	–	–	–	–	–	20,409
Total Assets	30,125	22,517	56,617	215,308	197,769	760,114	1,231,726	2,451,557
Liabilities and Capital								
Creditors	7,444	1,637	23,632	84,313	124,215	713,936	1,113,060	2,226,515
Reserve Fund	–	1,169	1,722	–	–	–	–	–
Subordinated Liabilities	–	–	–	–	–	–	47,879	87,559
Shareholders' Fund	22,681	19,711	31,263	130,995	73,554	46,178	70,787	137,483
	30,125	22,517	56,617	215,308	197,769	760,114	1,231,726	2,451,557

Appendix 5

Schedule of ICC Acts

Industrial Credit Act, 1933	Formation of Industrial Credit Company, Limited. Authorised Share Capital £5 million. Borrowing powers limited to amount of share capital.
Industrial Credit (Amendment) Act, 1958	Ministerial guarantees of £5 million authorised and extension of powers of Minister for Finance to acquire shares.
Industrial Credit (Amendment) Act, 1959	Authorised Share Capital increased to £10 million. Borrowing powers and Ministerial guarantees increased to £15 million. Minister empowered to make direct loans to ICC
Industrial Credit (Amendment) Act, 1971	Authorised Share Capital increased to £12 million. Borrowing powers and Ministerial guarantees increased to £30 million. ICC powers extended to cover the provision of finance outside Ireland provided it benefits Irish trade and industry.
Industrial Credit (Amendment) Act, 1974	Borrowing powers and Ministerial guarantees increased to £75 million.
Industrial Credit (Amendment) Act, 1977	Borrowing powers and Ministerial guarantees raised to £200 million.
Industrial Credit (Amendment) Act, 1979	Borrowing powers and Ministerial guarantees increased to £400 million.
Industrial Credit (Amendment) Act, 1983	Borrowing powers and Ministerial guarantees increased to £800 million. Number of directors increased from seven to nine.
Industrial Credit (Amendment) Act, 1990	Borrowing powers and Ministerial guarantees increased to £1 billion.
ICC Bank Act, 1992	Borrowing powers increased to £1.3 billion. Provision for supervision of the Company by the Central Bank. Removal of geographic and other restrictions on ICC's activities. Change of name to ICC Bank plc.
ICC Bank (Amendment) Act, 1997	Authorised Share Capital increased to £40 million. Borrowing powers increased to £2.3 billion.
ICC Bank Act, 1999	Borrowing powers increased to £3.5 billion. Provision for issue of shares in connection with an Employee Share Ownership Trust.

Bibliography

Andrews, C. S. (1982), *Man of No Property*, Dublin: The Mercier Press.

Anstead, M. (1999), 'Crying All the Way from the Bank', in *Director*, 52/10, pp. 38 – 42.

Barrington, T. J. (1980), *The Irish Administrative System*, Dublin: Institute of Public Administration.

Barry, F. (ed.), (1999), *Understanding Ireland's Economic Growth*, Basingstoke: Macmillan Press Limited.

Boskey, S. (1959), *Problems and Practices of Development Banks*, Baltimore: The Johns Hopkins University Press.

Clark, E. R. (1985), *The IDB – A History of Canada's Industrial Development Bank*, Toronto: University of Toronto Press.

Daly, M. E. (1992), *Industrial Development and Irish National Identity 1922-1939*, Dublin: Gill and Macmillan.

Diamond, W. (1957), *Development Banks*, Baltimore: The Johns Hopkins University Press.

Economic and Social Research Institute (ESRI), (1997), *Medium-Term Review, 1997–2003*, Dublin: ESRI.

Fanning, R. (1978), *The Irish Department of Finance, 1922-1958*, Dublin: Institute of Public Administration.

Finance, Department of, (1938), *Commission of Inquiry into Banking, Currency and Credit, 1938: Reports*, (Chairman: Joseph Brennan), Dublin: Stationery Office.

Finance, Department of, (1958), *Economic Development*, Dublin: Department of Finance.

Finance, Department of, (1958), *Programme for Economic Expansion; First*, Dublin: Stationery Office.

Finance, Department of, (Part I, 1963; Part II, 1964), *Programme for Economic Expansion; Second*, Dublin: Stationery Office.

Forfás, (1999), *Annual Employment Survey, 1998* Dublin: Forfás.

Hederman, M. (1983), *The Road to Europe* Dublin: Institute of Public Administration.

138

Industrial Credit Company, (1969), *Focus on Industrial Credit,* Dublin: The Industrial Credit Company Limited.

Industry and Commerce, Department of, (1992), *A Time for Change: Industrial Policy for the 1990s: Report of the Industrial Policy Review Group,* (Chairman: Jim Culliton), Dublin: Stationery Office.

Jones, I. F. (1974), *The Rise of a Merchant Bank: A Short History of Guinness Mahon,* Dublin: [Guinness & Mahon].

Keogh, D. (1994), *Twentieth-Century Ireland: Nation and State,* Dublin: Gill and Macmillan.

Kinross, J. (1982), *Fifty Years in the City: Financing Small Business,* London: John Murray.

Lee, J. J. (1989), *Ireland – 1912-1985,* Cambridge: Cambridge University Press.

McAleese, D. (1977), *A Profile of Grant-Aided Industry in Ireland,* Dublin: IDA Ireland.

McAleese, D. (ed.), (1989), *Competition and Industry – The Irish Experience,* Dublin: Gill and Macmillan.

McAleese, D. (1997-98), 'Economic Policy and Performance: The Irish Experience', in *Journal of the Statistical and Social Inquiry Society of Ireland,* XXVII/v, pp. 3 – 16.

McCague, E. (1994), *Arthur Cox, 1891-1965,* Dublin: Gill and Macmillan.

Morris, J. (1998), *Fifty Years of Europe: An Album,* Harmondsworth: Penguin Books.

Murray, C. H. (1990), *The Civil Service Observed,* Dublin: Institute of Public Administration.

National Economic and Social Council, (1982), *A Review of Industrial Policy: A Report prepared by the Telesis Consulting Group,* Dublin: National Economic and Social Council.

Ó Broin, L. (1982), *No Man's Man,* Dublin: Institute of Public Administration.

O'Farrell, P. N. (1975), *Regional Industrial Development Trends in Ireland 1960 – 1973,* Dublin: IDA Ireland.

Ó Gráda, C. (1997), *A Rocky Road – The Irish Economy since the 1920s,* Manchester: Manchester University Press.

Press, J. (1989), *The Footwear Industry in Ireland, 1922-1973,* Dublin: Irish Academic Press.

Réamonn, S. (1981), *History of the Revenue Commissioners,* Dublin: Institute of Public Administration.

Share, B. (1986) *The Flight of the Iolar: The Aer Lingus Experience,* Dublin: Gill and Macmillan

Share, B. (1999), *The Quarrymen – The Roadstone Story 1949-1999,* Dublin: Roadstone.

Thomas, W. A. (1986), *The Stock Exchanges of Ireland,* Liverpool: Francis Cairns (Publications) Limited.

Verolme, C. (1975), *Verolme Memoir,* Rotterdam: Ad. Danker.

Whelan, S. (1999), *From Canals to Computers,* Dublin: Friends First Asset Management.

Whitaker, T. K. (1983), *Interests,* Dublin: Institute of Public Administration.

White, D. (1998), *A Century of Banking,* Dublin: The Institute of Bankers in Ireland.

Index